Growing Your Highly Profitable Face Painting Business

Sherrill Church

Mimicks Face Painting

Growing Your
Highly Profitable
Face Painting Business

ISBN   978 0 9576265 1 5

First Edition 2013 Great Britain

Copyright ©2013 Sherrill Church

Published by Mimicks

DEDICATION

This book is dedicated simply to
everyone who ever told me that
you can't make any money with
face painting!

CONTENTS

Chapter 7 – Adding Immense Value

Chapter 8 – How Are You Selling Yourself?

Chapter 9 – Setting Your Prices

Chapter 10 – How To Write a Business Plan

Chapter 11 – Marketing Your Business

Resources

ACKNOWLEDGMENTS

Mimicks Face Painting has been on a long journey over the past two decades and without the commitment and dedication of employed staff it wouldn't have been possible. So I'd like to thank:

Jo, Cathy, Nicole, Anna, Katie, Rachel, Natalie, Clare, Lucy, Emma, Kellie, Rachel, Carol, Emma, Beckie, Aimee, Sue, Natalie, Louise, Erica, Lian, Beckie, Hayley, Sarah, Amy, Reema, Vicky, Gemma, Vanessa, Kayleigh, Charlotte, Ashmi, Sam, Tara, Jayne, Kerrie, Marie, Rachel, Megan, Victoria, Sam, Leanne, Emily, Louise, Emma, Chloe, Vicki, Ruth, Becca, Emma, Anna, Tania, Kelly, Hayley, Avaneet, Stephanie, Phillipa, Helen, Keri, Kayleigh

....and the biggest acknowledgement and thanks go to
Roger my husband, Ashlea my daughter and Brenda my mum

Oh and of course my much loved son who spent many a weekend on his own fending for himself because his mother was in a field in a different part of the country somewhere. Thank you Asa for looking after the cat!

CHAPTER 1

Invest In Yourself

Kick Start Your Company

Welcome to .... Growing Your Own Profitable Face Painting Business. So you want to have a more lucrative face painting business do you? Well the book you're holding here in your hands is going to help you to have just that.

Becoming a truly successful face painter running a very profitable business is purely a matter of decision. In a nutshell – it's *you* who will decide on just how successful *you* will be. It's your decision. Whether you succeed or fail in business is entirely up to *you* and is a result of the decisions that you make on a daily basis. It will be your decision to go at it full throttle to make some serious money or it will be up to you to you make the decision to just sit back and hope and pray that your next big break (or booking contract) will land on your lap without any effort on your part.

Hundreds of face painters join our industry every year. They don't think twice about buying an endless amount of products for their kit, sometimes spending a small fortune in doing so. And with these new face paints, sparkly glitters and brushes they practise and perfect their skills over a considerable amount of time and they then do the occasional events and birthday parties. But what next? Face painters can easily spend a couple of hundred pounds in the first few months of running their business on plenty of kit and equipment items, but most don't spend any money on investment in themselves. Yeah sure they'll buy design books and magazines providing them with much needed inspiration on how to do their actual face painting designs ..... but what about the business side, the self-promotion, building their customer list, their marketing activities, securing customer relationships and actually running their business as a business and not just winging their way through. Sadly, not an influential business book to be seen on their bookshelf. Investment in knowledge is what makes the business world go round and with a whole stack-load of the latest must-have face painting kit is not going to be enough to succeed in this industry. Simple as that!

You, on the other hand, have taken a huge positive step in the right direction. You've bought this book because you want to know how to really run a profitable face painting venture. You want to feed your mind with the business principles and strategies that have already proven to be successful from someone like me who's been there, done that, worn the t-shirt and now written the book. By implementing the many tactics that are ready and waiting for you over the following pages that are transferable straight from my face painting business right smack-bang into your face painting business, you won't have to go out and re-invent the wheel. Stealing established information is a lot faster and easier and more likely to generate success.

To reach a higher level of success in your business you should be consistently investing in yourself. Not only investing in the latest must-have products and kit that may well enhance your creative skill, but also investing in your business knowledge. You're not going to reach your true income potential by just having the latest and greatest face painting product to hit the market. You need to be feeding your mind with business strategies from a variety of sources and not just your own industry.

The businesses that I've run have all grown through investment in my knowledge – the books I've read, the people I've met, the courses I've attended. I've spent over a thousand pounds alone on business books and have quite a comprehensive and diverse collection, all of which help to feed my mind and provide the fuel and inspiration to become as successful as I possibly can. In my spare time I've usually got my head stuck into a business book of some sort, eager to learn, eager to try new ways of doing things and eager to become inspired by the greatest of entrepreneurs. This investment in my-self has been well worth it and has paid for itself time and time again. The saying is so true – 'Poor people have large televisions, and wealthy people have large libraries'!

This investment in you starts here and now. So before you settle into this book, grab yourself a notebook and pen as there will be plenty of 'Ah-ha, now that's a good idea' moments for you to write down as and when they happen.

So let's crack on –
It's time to kick-start *your* face painting company.

CHAPTER 2

Taking Consistent Action In Key Business Areas

Let's Make Some Lists

A number one priority in running a successful business is to have plenty of ideas that you'd like to implement into your business. After all, we're creative people aren't we and we have tonnes of ideas. Those ideas, dreams, hopes and desires (or whatever you'd like to call them) need to be documented into action plans, and those actions plans usually start out as lists. So let's organise your business and make some lists.

Oh how I love lists! You can never have enough lists. I have lists for everything –shopping lists, work lists, phone call lists, books to read lists, lists of lists to write lists, and lists of jobs for the hubby and the kids to do as well. I grew up with lists, as my parents were great believers in them. Everything went on a list so you didn't (couldn't) forget. Even now I often hear my Mum say "Have you put that on your list"!

My lists initially start life on scrappy pieces of paper – well maybe not so much of the scrappy as I do use A4 sheets that have been torn into quarters and bulldog clipped together into a pad. If I didn't have these paper pads to hand strategically positioned around my home then fleeting ideas and inspirational moments would come and go as I've got a memory like a sieve and if I don't write a note or a put it on a list it's here today gone the next minute. These scribbled thoughts are then transferred into their relevant action plan folders – of which I have many.

When running any type of business, lists will be crucial to the everyday planning and administration. Without daily, weekly and monthly action plans (lists) you may find that business growth is pretty much at a standstill and not really moving forward. By keeping a focused eye on the tasks and projects in hand will help towards the planning of your future success – even if your future is simply tomorrow.

When you set out on a long road trip you may use a traditional map or a Sat-Nav as it's usual to plan your route and know what resources you'll need in advance. Business practice is no different. If you're unclear from the start about which road to follow it will take you a lot longer to get to your desired destination.

Let's start by putting your lists into priority order so that you can become more organized with your time management. You need to think about absolutely everything that you want to do and need to do in your business this week, next month and for the year ahead. But first before you can schedule in any of those business commitments you need to make a list of where all your time is actually being spent now – your priority activities on this list should include most of the following aspects:

- Time to focus on your other employment (if applicable).
- Time to get ready and prepare for work.
- Time with your spouse or partner.
- Time with your children.
- Time with your family.
- Time for grocery shopping and other shopping trips.
- Time to socialize with your friends.
- Time for housework and other domestic obligations.
- Time to exercise.
- Time to read.
- Time to relax and chill out.
- Time for short breaks and holidays.
- Time to sleep – ah!

After you've made your list to include all the priorities above and any other extra bits and bobs you may wish to add that I've not included, you'll probably find that it's already quite extensive. Next I suggest you purchase an appointment book that has time-slots in it – a bit like the ones that hair dressers and beauty therapists use in salons, and then you can set about putting all your regular un-business related activities into it from the list you've just made above, placing each one into its relevant time-slot. Choose to do this over a 3-month time-span. Also remember to schedule in some empty time and some quality time as well. After those priority activities have been added in and of course any other employment that you may have, next add in all of your face painting events and commitments that you have booked in.

Decide what else is important in your life and include it by diarising in those things of importance, making sure that they're scheduled in well in advance, like holidays and short-breaks. You must also include any other commitments and disruptions that can be a big distraction to your business life, which may be quite different from the list above, but if it's stuff you have to do, it has to go on your list! Maybe you need to think long and hard about how you could minimise any of those disruptions and turn them into effective strategies by putting them to good use.

From here you'll be able to see at a glance your available daily time and you can now start to block out hourly sections of each day that you're going to dedicate to your business growth and administration, which is paramount to your business success. You'll be able to use your appointment book as a guide to your time which will enable you to put it to much better effect. This will give you a clearer picture of how much actual time can be devoted to your face painting business. If it turns out that you only have 14 spare hours a week available scattered throughout the seven days then you must make sure that you use those 14 hours effectively and prioritise each week by only doing actions that are going to be business building principles that will get you moving forward. Don't waste those valuable 14 hours doing un-necessary things that will only keep your business stagnant without any growth.

If you haven't yet got yourself an appointment book you can type out some daily spreadsheets with time-slots and then start to add all your actions into the sheets over the next six-weeks. This exercise will give you a clearer picture of your time management by outlining your available hours that you have so that you can work on your business.

Organizing Your Lists

So now you'll have a clearer picture of your available hours that you can devote to your business growth. Each day of the week may be different, some may have only 2 spare hours a day, others may have more and some may have none. Either way you'll now be able to see what time blocks you have stretched out in front of you to fit in your business tasks and actions.

If you have a stack of 'to do' lists, looking at them can be a daunting prospect as everything on those lists seems to be a priority. Not so, as many tasks can be put on the back burner and re-scheduled for another day. It's all about prioritising and scheduling. You'll need some sort of order to the everyday chaos that your 'to do' lists can produce. Are your lists easy to find or are they spread over many single pieces of paper and post-it notes that are tucked away in drawers, stuck on the fridge or hidden under the bread bin, which serves as a reminder of how unorganised you may be! Your list may be a mile long or a simple one-page sheet, but either way it needs prioritising and scheduling.

Okay, so let's organise your lists. These are the ones with your ideas on and all the things that you need to do that are possibly written down onto countless pieces of paper. We'll put them into daily plans, weekly plans and monthly plans:

Daily Action Plans – You can produce daily time-sheets easily with a word processor using a table format, producing one for each day of the week. At the top of the page add a heading and a sub-heading that says:

To Do Today

Monday 3rd February – 3 Business Admin Hours

Format your table with 10 rows and 2 columns, making the left-hand column quite small and the right-hand column large. The column to the left will be for you to add time-scales into and the right-hand column will be space for the task itself. Spread your 10 lines out evenly down the page so they end up as nice large boxes.

Next print out seven daily time sheets that indicate your available time-spans and start to write in all the business tasks that you'll like to work on or achieve this coming week. It may include things like design a new leaflet, telephone a handful of previous customers or book some trade events.

This is the time sheet system that I use which works so very well for me. On it I write everything that is a priority to do today in black pen and everything else that's not quite so important I write in blue pen. I also have space at the bottom of the page to write down in green pen some of the un-business related jobs that will also need doing like walking the dogs, nipping to the shops and doing the ironing. By doing this I'm able to see my day ahead at a glance. Ten lined boxes is usually more than enough as it's wise to remember not to be over ambitious by entering too much work to do each day or over the forth-coming week. It can be very disheartening when you get to Friday and you see how many of those business tasks are still left on your time-sheets that you didn't achieve which will end up leaving you feeling very despondent.

Once a task is achieved I then strike it through with a highlighter pen and it gives me great satisfaction if I can cross off two or three all at once!

To make your daily time sheet even more organised you could list the expected time needed for each task in the small column on the left of your table and then write each task into a specific time slot. This is being very strict and will also help you with any over-running on things that are taking up too much of your time that you can put a halt to. I have recently found a great little resource on the Internet – a stop watch that you can have displayed on the desktop of your computer which will ring out at the time you have set it to ring. So no more spending too long on time-sapping stuff and it's especially beneficial to use when you are visiting forums or checking your email inbox as those are the moments when time seems to just fly by. It can be found at http://www.online-stopwatch.com

I usually plan my daily time sheets out on a Sunday evening so that the following week is clearly laid out in a structured format and one that is easy to follow enabling me to see my week ahead at a glance. Yeah okay you may say it's a little bit on the OCD side – but hey that's just me being totally organized as usual!

Weekly Action Plans – For these action plans I have an A4 ring binder with section dividers. Each divider is labelled with specific tasks that I am currently working on. For example: website updates, email campaigns, adverts to be placed, customers to be contacted, and so on and so on.

When I'm planning my working week I flick through this folder and I add anything of priority from it to my daily time-sheets. I choose the priorities first that are wealth creation; these are the ones that will reap the most benefits bringing money into my business, like adding new service information to my website. If it's not a priority or wealth creation it can wait another week or so.

With all your pending projects, tasks or whatever you choose to call them and your new business ideas stored neatly in this folder will give you a clearer picture of what you need to get through over the coming weeks. You can either tackle each one in sequence making sure that it's just right before going onto the next project or you can multi-task and have your fingers in lots of projects all at once! I hope you'll do the latter as you should try to work on several different projects all at once - simultaneously. Simultaneous action means taking action in all of the important business areas as soon as they arise and not just concentrating on one project or task over a length of time. Obviously some will take more priority over others, but doing several things at once and avoiding excuses for not taking action, greatness will emerge – even if it has an element of chaos to it. If you put all of your time and energy into one project and it became a failure (and you'll get plenty of them) you would have wasted hours, weeks even months that could have been put to better use. This does however include an aspect of pandemonium – but a great way to work as better things will materialize by working on a few projects all at once.

Monthly Action Plans – This is the big project folder, which again has section dividers. This is where the meaty stuff goes that needs forward planning and scheduling, things that I know will take a considerable amount of time and resources.

In here will be ideas, notes and information on things like updating my customer database, sending out mail-shots and writing sales letters, working on new services and promotions, and setting my six-monthly marketing plan, etc. This folder is looked at intermittently and projects from it are moved into the weekly folder and from there they are then allocated space on the daily time sheets. If at any time you find that your monthly folder is bursting at the seams, then it could be time to start thinking about delegating some of your projects to family, close friends or even recruiting an assistant to help you. I've had some wonderful assistants over the years and they have been so valuable in the office taking care of the commonplace tasks such as sending out confirmations and invoices to customers which frees up my time immensely leaving me to work on the marketing side of the business and not always on the administration side of the business.

With your new ideas for business growth now safely written onto your lists in this folder they can be mulled over, built upon, tweaked and launched straight into your marketing plan.

Now you may find this next action of mine a bit strange but I never screw up used pieces of paper before putting them in the bin as I get great satisfaction from tearing them up into as many pieces as I can after a list is obsolete. Great satisfaction. It's the little things in life that pleases me. My bin looks like a confetti explosion. Incidentally did you know that you can't tear a sheet of paper no matter what size it is more than eight times (a useless bit of information there I know)!

All in all, quite a comprehensive system that works most efficiently for my face painting business. I have tried many things over the years and you too will eventually find a system that works well for you and your scheduled priorities, and when you do – stick to it and run with it with a vengeance.

Unfortunately we are conditioned to take one step at a time which is okay for some tasks and aspects of life, but not always so good for the small business owner. If we did just one action at a time and saw it through to its finished result our business would grow and move forward at a snail's pace. You need to be conditioned to move with speed like the rabbit and race along with bursting energy, multi-tasking on a variety of projects all at once. If you work on three new things to get customers all at the same time rather than just working on one thing, it will triple your effectiveness and you'll get results that much faster.

Putting ideas, tasks and projects into practice and actually doing them is so, so, so important. Remember that it's the doing that's going to make you money.

Are You Analyzing Your Results

You may already be aware of the 80/20 principle and how it relates to everything in our life, whether that's material or immaterial. In a nutshell the formula is that 80% of your results have come from 20% of your effort? This is known at the 80/20 principle and recently I've read some great books on this subject, especially the book by Richard Koch, and to be honest I'm converted.

Judge this for yourself. Over the next working week analyse your daily time-sheets looking at all your actions and their individual time-scales. Next analyze the effectiveness of what you did by taking a highlighter pen, say a pink one and striking through every activity that added value to your business and would put money in the bank. Next take a different coloured pen, say a blue one and highlight everything that was a necessary daily task to do, like the school run. Now drastically strike through with a yellow highlighter anything that was a complete waste of your time.

You now have some statistics =
o Pink – Do more of, again and again
o Blue – Maybe delegate to someone else
o Yellow – Stop doing

Pink is probably about 20% and Blue and Yellow are about 80%. So you need to more of the pink stuff which is going to turn into profits.

Looking at your charts you will find that only about 20% of your time is actually spent making money, which could be so much better. You need to do so much more of the 20% in order to move your business forward to its next level. Take a look at the remaining 80% and make a decision about how you can delegate these necessary tasks and how you can prevent yourself from doing totally ineffective things each and every day.

Developing Your Action Habit

There's an explicit element to success that most business owners never truly grasp, let alone come close to creating the financial results that they desire. It relates to their ability to take *constant action*. Not one of any brilliant ideas that you may have will be worth a penny unless you take positive significant action. By focusing on your actions will be directly related to your income and profits. Being able to cultivate your ideas and beliefs is a crucial activity for your business growth.

Developing the action habit takes some self-control as quite often we may think that we are really busy, but if fact what we are doing is in fact a waste of time. How often at the end of your day (when you're not providing your face painting service but working on your business) do you feel completely satisfied with all that you have accomplished? Be honest. Do you sit there in the twilight hours reflecting on your day's work and think to yourself "Well I didn't really do that much today did I, not when you consider the hours I put in"? This is called analysis paralysis. Too much thinking time and not enough doing time, faffing around so to speak. As someone once said "He who hesitates is lost". One of the biggest barriers to success is hesitation.

Most of your time may be filled up with daily drudge, unnecessary actions and highly ineffective use of the few hours that you may have. You may realise it even more so after doing the daily time sheets exercise! It's common practice to feel busy, to feel like you're achieving, but when it boils down to it and you reflect back, you're probably just (you got it) busy being busy.

Maybe you use the well known "I'm too busy excuse" to avoid taking important actions such as implementing new marketing strategies. You should set yourself a discipline to do one marketing activity every day that will lead to money in the bank – and turn that into a habit. There are probably a handful of actions that you could have taken that are probably a dozen times more effective and profitable than anything else. Focus on doing whatever it takes to remove the ineffective uses of your time and you'll see a direct impact on your growth and profits. Overcoming hesitation and taking substantial simultaneous action is both energizing and very financially rewarding.

I've also discovered that good enough is good enough. Being in the industry that we're in, we all tend to be perfectionists, which of course is very important for the face painting service that we provide to our customers, but not so good for our business growth. It's far better to get a project going and getting it out there even if it's not quite as perfect as it could be (an unfinished website as an example) than to play around with it, tweaking it, adding to it when it was basically already good enough. Perfection can come later – launching it as 'good enough' comes first. I'd hate to add up all those lost hours I spent just playing around with things trying to make them perfect when they were already good enough. Such things spring to mind like tweaking photographs on a promotional leaflet making sure they were cropped to perfection, pixel by pixel and changing font styles and sizes just to see which one of the 30 on the short list looked better!!!! What an absolute waste of business input time. Actually I have also wasted a lot of unnecessary time on writing this book – tweaking it here, tweaking it there, generally fine-tuning it. I probably could have launched it two years earlier if I hadn't faffed around with it so much!

It's all very well having a list of actions, time sheets and project folders at the ready and having goals set and business plans in place (more on business planning in a while) if you're not going to act on them. Actions speak louder than words. You, and only you, need to make it happen! Putting things into practice and actually doing them is so important. And like I said above it's the doing that's going to make you money. Unfortunately success doesn't come knocking on your door, looking for you. It won't break your door down and insist on coming in. You have to go after it. Decide what is important in your life and include it in your time plans. Include things of importance and make sure they are scheduled into your diary – well in advance.

CHAPTER 3

Positive Thinking

Is Your Glass Half Full or Half Empty?

Positive thinking is a really significant aspect for your business success. You need to have a great attitude and mind set all the time which will help you through the hard times and how you deal with things is what will make all the difference. Your positive attitude will rub off onto your customers as will equally a bad attitude. There indeed will be times when your glass is half empty, and it's on those not so good occasions that you must flip the balance by looking on the bright side, find the good elements of the situation and strive for a more positive outlook.

You can turn other business peoples' behaviour patterns into a beneficial and positive format for the success of your own business. Think about those who have arrived at the place in the business world or in the face painting industry where you want to be and get your behaviour patterns to match with theirs and a most important change will happen to speed your business progress up to the next level. You should model yourself on other people's successes. Literally choose any person in business, any business that inspires you no matter how big or small, that gives you motivation and that you would love to replicate. Make a study on them by gaining as much information as possible by looking at their website, their sales literature and speaking with their customers if you can. Don't try to re-write their formula and re-invent the wheel because if it works for them then make it work for you. Become a magpie and feather your own nest with little bits and bobs from others that have inspired you.

To help you to get into a positive mindset every morning pick up a success related book and read it for about 5 minutes. That's all – just 5 minutes. You could even do this before you actually get out of bed. Soak up any positive ideas that you could implement into your business life and these ideas will be embedded into your sub-conscious. You'll be uplifted from the start of the day and you'll start to develop habits similar to those who you read about. Read as much as you can on a daily basis and fill your mind with vital material to sift and sort through. You can experiment with this by reading different and various view-points, diverse success biographies, business books and marketing publications. How many times have your read through a face painting or make-up trade magazine and thought to yourself "I could do that". Business books and biographies will also instil the same positive attitude for you. Become inspired on a regular basis.

When you read a good book that inspires you, as you read through highlight all the points of interest and all the things you want to remember. After you've read the book go back over all the highlighted points and write them down on paper adding your own ideas and thoughts. Next type it all out and this will further embed it into your memory and reinforce your learning by three-times. Once on the first reading, secondly going back and hand-writing out all your highlighted points and thirdly by typing it out into a word-processor. Reinforce, reinforce, reinforce. It's a fantastic way of remembering things and something that I do quite often. If you have a selection of business books, celebrity biographies and trade magazines make a list of all the titles. Next to each title on your list write a brief sentence of what elements in the book or magazine you could use as a pick-me-up, something to inspire you. For instance a trade magazine will get your creative juices flowing, a business book will give you a positive mindset and a biography will motivate you to become great at what you do.

Hopes and Dreams

We all have hopes and dreams, maybe for a better life or a person we aspire to be. Maybe we want to be healthier, fitter, wealthier or more loved. You have to have hopes and dreams as this will give you something tangible to work towards. Build a portfolio of your desires and call it 'I want it, I deserve it and I will get it'. Positive thinking followed by positive documentation then positive actions leads to positive outcomes.

There will be occasions when you will be up to your neck in the stresses and the strains of organising and running your face painting business and negativity may creep it. Don't worry – it happens to all of us. This is the time you should sit back, clear your mind and re-evaluate the reasons why you are in business and concentrate on thoughts that are positive and productive. This is so important as time to time you will have challenges and obstacles to overcome.

Get yourself into a better mood, pick up that inspiring book and synchronise yourself positively with your business – mentally, emotionally and behaviourally.

- Mentally – feed your mind with positive thoughts by reading articles and publications that will inspire you.

- Emotionally - book onto the next face painting jam or convention where you can rub shoulders with like-minded individuals and become totally stimulated.

- Behaviourally – do something positive like design a handful of new face painting designs for your display board.

Don't let any outside causes determine your business success for you as negative influences can paralyse you with fear. Whatever effect is about to happen or is happening it will be all too easy for you to blame your upbringing, where you live, the government, the media, or the economy for a failing business. Rise above any negativity that meets you face to face whether that is economic coverage in the news, friends voicing their negative opinions about how you should get a 'proper job' and family members trying to be of help but who are all too often putting doubt in your mind that you'll ever make a success as a face painter as it's not a 'real career'. If it wasn't a real job or career then why have I been successfully running Mimicks for well over two decades now!

Maybe you have negative influences that are affecting you at the moment, whether personal like a friend pooh-poohing your business venture, or a business related issue like a new face painter targeting your market? Implement positive ways in which to run your business and stop worrying and listening to others who harp on about negative influences and all too easily are ready to place blame on others. All of these negativities can infuse a fear of failure before you even get off the ground if you let them. You need to change your mind set and become optimistic, positive and forward thinking in everything you to on a daily basis. Shift gear into a more positive outlook and then look in the mirror and say out loud what it is you want to achieve, and say it often. As you sharpen your positive attitude you'll not only find that you'll rise above all the negative influences and possible criticism but you will leave all those non-believers standing there with their mouths wide-open!

A few years ago I found myself in a very negative place (which is most unusual for me) when my party venue was up for sale for many months. I needed to sell the business as a going concern as the shop lease was entering its break-clause and I needed to pass the business on before it expired. I read 'The Secret' and other books about positive attraction and it completely changed my mindset on how i viewed the sale of my business and within a very short time-scale the business sold.

You can also plan to make any negative situations that may arise into positive ones. Think seriously about what would happen if certain situations crept into your business life that you had little or no control over. What would happen if you lost your bookings diary, what would happen if you had a flood or fire at home, what would happen if your key staff member left if you had one, what would happen if you had a cash flow crisis, what would happen if you broke your wrist on your painting hand, your website crashes, your telephone is cut off, your partner walks out, someone steals your car with all your kit and equipment in it, or recession hits you really badly. WOW – that's a big list of negative situations.

You need to put contingency action plans and policies into place, and you need to put them into place now. Don't ever say "Oh that won't happen to me", or "That's not important for me to do yet" because the unexpected has a way of creeping up to bite us on the bum when we least expect it. So be warned – backup your computer documents today!! I think I better repeat that – back up your computer documents today.

Get Positive Today

So on the positive side and with your positive attitude you also need strong belief, confidence, desire, willpower, commitment and enthusiasm. Enthusiasm comes from the heart and it's very infectious. You're the only one that can make things happen in your business. Quite often I hear my customers say to me 'You're always so happy, you've got such a positive outlook'. Absolutely. There's no reason at all that you can't inspire the people that you come into contact with on a daily basis. Your positive thoughts will lead to strategy building, which in turn leads to implementation which leads to speed which builds momentum which leads to magnetism which leads to wealth in your business.

So here's a formula for success which you should write out in large words on a piece of card and stick it where you'll see it every day (by your computer, by your bed, in the downstairs loo, wherever)

→ Positive Thinking: Look for positive opportunities
  → Positive Opportunities: Build your future plans
    → Implementation: Putting those plans into action
      → Building Momentum: The habit will gather speed
        → Magnetism: Speed attracts good things to you
          → Wealth in Your Business: Goal

Get positive today and everyday – it's highly infectious.

CHAPTER 4

Your Target Market

Is Anyone There?

When choosing your service to provide, or product to sell, it's important to be sure that there is a market for it and that it is something that customers will want to buy from you. You need to find out what people are spending their money on in the face painting industry and do what it takes to maximise on it. This customer will then become your Target Market.

You need to appeal to a perceptive sector of the market as you cannot possibly sell to everyone and there will only be a proportion of people interested in what you're offering. Don't make the mistake of trying to market to everybody. Look for gaps and opportunities in the market place and exploit them if you can and this means spotting trends as they happen.

By having a basic understanding of who your customer is will help you with your marketing plan, and by having an array of information on them will make it easier to sell to them. What they all have in common will allow you to target new customers more easily and you can then direct your marketing into that specific category, rather than going in blind and mailing to the masses or placing adverts in totally irrelevant publications. Right from the very beginning, if you don't know who your target market is you're setting yourself up for failure. By knowing who they are will help you to sharpen up your marketing and you'll be able to communicate it more effectively to that specific group of people.

So who is your ideal customer? Who is your business for? What is their general profile? What do they all have in common? Think about it now. Find out about the type of customer you want to sell to and push your marketing in their direction.

To find out about your customer profile and their common traits, which is also known as a niche, you'll need to do some sort of survey, which is always easier to do on *existing* customers if you already have them, than on those who are your potential customers. Once you have researched who your niche is and what their similar characteristics and requirements are, will allow you to tailor your services to meet their particular needs, as you will find that these common traits will lead to similar buying decisions from other like-minded individuals.

So Who is Your Target Market?

You can understand who your target market is by doing some research on them. A great way to capture this information is just through general conversation with your existing customers and after the event making notes of your findings. This will be a great help towards your marketing efforts as you'll be better informed where to focus your efforts and attention on.

Your face painting customers will fall into two different segmentations of target market. Segment one will consist of Private Consumers (PC's) who book you to attend birthday parties, family occasions and the like. Segment two will consist of businesses and corporations who book your services on a Business to Business basis (B2B).

Below is a generalised list of all the different types of research information that you can collect on your target market to better understand them. I've put in which segment of your market they refer to by using PC and B2B.

- Home – What type of house do they live in? Is it on an estate, or in a village, is it in the city, or maybe a remote dwelling in the country? How many bedrooms, bathrooms and reception rooms does it have? PC.

- Area – Are you able to locate your target market easily? Where do they live, and in what type of area? How far are you willing to travel to get to them to provide your face painting service? PC & B2B.

- Marital Status – What is their circumstance with regards to their relationships? Are they single, in a partnership, married or divorced? PC.

- Family - How many children do they have, how many girls and how many boys, and what are their ages? Are they school age children or in further education. In what environment did they gain their education, independent or mainstream? PC.

- Class - Is their social standing important? Are they from the lower to middle class bracket or are they the high class and affluent type where money is no object and they don't buy on price alone? Maybe they are blue-chip companies. PC & B2B.

- Car - What type of car do they drive? Is it from an inexpensive range which could pre-dispose them to just making do, or do they drive a prestige car and expect all the quality and luxuries that they have come to know and expect? PC.

- Groceries – Do they buy their groceries from a large National multi-chain supermarket or do they frequently use the small independent shop for their weekly goods, which will also include personal service? PC.

- Clothes - Where do they shop for their clothes? Can they usually be seen as a patron to designer shops in affluent locations, or the mainstream stores in shopping centres, or is their usual shopping spree done on the Internet? PC.

- Tabloids - What newspapers do they read and is this on a daily or weekly basis. What are their favourite

SHERRILL CHURCH | Mimicks Face Painting

consumer magazines or trade publications, and what triggers them to purchase that particular publication? PC & B2B.

- Self Esteem - Will your service touch on a psychological factor for them? Could your service appeal to those wishing to be seen to always have the best of everything? PC & B2B.

- Lifestyle – Will your service relate to a certain type of lifestyle? Does your target market like to 'keep up with the Joneses' or do they like to set a new trend in motion being the first to try something new and fashionable? PC & B2B.

- Price - Are they price conscious and only buy on price alone, always looking for the cheapest option, or do they understand that price can be a reflection of the quality of service that is provided and value for money? PC & B2B.

- Frequency - Will they use your service on a regular and consistent basis and become a long-standing loyal customer which is most certainly the type you want, or will they be here today and gone tomorrow with a one-off isolated event booking? B2B.

- Networking - Do they belong to any groups, clubs or alliances that you can also join in order to get close to them? Can you get to know them by visiting and participating in certain types of forums, such as NetMums? PC & B2B.

- Social Media - Do they frequently visit social media sites, if so, which ones and how often? How many followers and friends do they have on there which could also potentially be your target market? PC & B2B.

So who is your ideal customer? What's their profile? What are their common traits? Are you able to do a survey to find out?

Compiling the above information will take a considerable amount of time and effort, and once in receipt of that information you will need to place it into a database of some sort so that it can be added to as new people become your customers and reviewed on a regular basis. An Excel document is always a good place for storage of such details as is a table format in a Word processor. Failing that a simple hand-drafted document would suffice. Once you have a clear picture of whom your potential customer is, it is quite possible to purchase a list of customers in your area with the same matching qualities as your target, should you wish to pursue that route.

When working in customer's homes keep an eye out for items that could build their profile. Things like newspapers, magazines and used shopping bags. Also make a mental note of the type of car they drive and the classification of the area in which they live. All these things will help you to understand your customer profile better.

By undertaking a thorough market research will enable you to target your customer more effectively with regards to your advertising both online and offline, it will provide you with priorities regarding your networking activities, and will assist in the design of your sales and promotional literature. For example, the quality of your brochure – does it need to be a super high-class glossy one or will a standardised cheaper version do. If you're attending a lot of parties for wealthy customers you most certainly don't want hand-made computer based leaflets to hand out at the end of the event. Instead go for nice glossy printed ones that have been professionally designed and printed. There are many ways that you can get your message across, however you must ensure that you go about it in a cost-effective way. Spending your hard-earned cash on marketing activities should be measured and calculated so that you don't fall into the trap of over-spending on say an advertising campaign that has little or no response from your target market by advertising in completely the wrong type of publication. The overall cost of your communication should be checked and calculated against how much income was generated from responses and how much profit went into the bank.

If you happen to be at the start-up stage in your face painting business whereby you don't have any customers and are therefore unable to work out their common profile you can research your target market by talking and listening to other allied industries. Make an acquaintance with other entertainers in your area and this way you will be able to glean the information needed in order to build your customer profile.

You'll find that most small business owners love to talk about themselves and about how their business is doing (or not doing!). This will give you valuable information that you can use to identify your potential customer.

You will no doubt be in competition with other face painters in your area, and the mere fact that this competition exists should not worry or deter you. Competition is healthy, as they say, and it means that there is a ready and willing audience for you to market to, you just need to be able to offer your customers some sort of extra value to your service provision.

Eventually you'll find the type of customer that you actually love to be of service to, you know the type …. plenty of repeat bookings, money no object, always completely satisfied, etc. Well the way to get more of the type of customer who you consider to be a perfect match is to look at who this customer is, where they came from and how they came to you. Perhaps it was through a referral, maybe from a leaflet you placed at a certain establishment or maybe from an advert you placed in a particular magazine. By knowing how your customer come to be will help you in leaps and bounds to attract the same or similar sort. Create a spreadsheet to record where your customers came from and review it often. Find out what marketing element is working for you and what's not, and do more of the stuff that's bringing in your ideal customer.

CHAPTER 5

Customer Needs

What Does Your Customer Really Want?

Once you understand your customer profile and just who your target market is, the next stage is to market your service or product to them in such a way that what you offer is so irresistible to them that they just can't refuse your offer.

To do this effectively you will need to become perceptive to your customers needs, wants and desires. Needs, wants and desires are at the forefront of all business sales. If your customer doesn't want it, doesn't need it or doesn't desire it – then they simply will not buy it. It's as easy as that!

Let's take a closer look at needs, wants and desires:

- A Need – is a requirement or necessity of something in need or something that requires a course of action, as in help.

- A Want – can be a wish for something, or something to be attended to in a specified way.

- A Desire – is a request for an unsatisfied longing or craving, as in a heart's desire for something.

Some examples of your customer's needs, wants and desires could be:

- The PC customer *needs* to have face painting at their event in order to keeps the kids amused and entertained.

- The B2B customer *wants* the face painting activity to draw in the crowds so that company sales can be made at their shop launch/promotion/sale.

- The customer *desires* to have their face painted (or their child's face painted) at an event because they've always wanted to have it done but have never had the ideal opportunity to do so.

We usually find that needs and wants arise from a problematic situation. In other words, your customer has a problem that she would like you to solve. She can't possibly put on a party for 20 hyper 6-year olds without having some sort of entertainment in place. She doesn't want to spend the complete party entertaining the children because she needs to be entertaining all the parents that are staying for the duration. By looking for the problems that your customers are experiencing will enable you to understand their needs, wants and desires and this in turn will be the key to targeting your market with a service or product that becomes an enticing offer.

In order to sell a product or service to a customer is all about getting inside their heads and really understanding what makes them tick. What problem can you solve for them by providing your face painting service? What needs will they have when you are actually doing the service to either a party mum or a corporate booker? What desire of theirs will you be able to fulfil prior to the event, during the event and after the event? Your customer will be looking for reassurance of quality and professionalism from someone else who can take control of the circumstances.

People don't just buy for the sake of it. There is always an underlying problem to be solved, or a need or a want or a desire to be realised. Take these additional points as an example:

- People purchase a car because they don't want to walk
- People book a window cleaner because they don't want to clean their own windows
- People go on holiday because they deserve a well-earned break
- People buy expensive shoes because they desire to look well groomed
- People buy a new coat because the winter is coming and they need to be warm
- People buy anti-ageing skin care because they want their wrinkles to disappear
- People buy food and water because they want to live

. . . and the list could go on and on and on!

Every service or product that is purchased is generally done so to fulfil needs, wants, desires and problems.

Go one step further and think about all the services that you have used over the past month and write them down. Now attach a need, a want, a desire or a problem to them all. Do the same for your monthly purchases, everything you spent your hard-earned cash on even if you only bought it on a whim (at the time you must have thought you had a need for it)! It's a great little exercise to do because it really does highlight the necessity on how you can attract your clients by identifying what it is they actually want from you

Are You Really Interested In Your Customer?

Start becoming genuinely interested in other people and what they have to say, either to you or to other people. In other words, become a professional eavesdropper! Listen out for needs, wants and desires and act on them as soon as you can. Is there something that you can offer them, can you help in anyway. Think of an angle. I make a habit of listening in to others people's conversations; especially Mum's waiting in the face painting queue and especially when they're chatting about previous entertainment experiences. I make a mental note of their unfulfilled needs that they talk of and work on a way that I can use it to my marketing advantage.

There are certain words that you need to listen out for. As soon as you hear the sentence starters listed below, you need to adjust your concentration level and prick-up your radar.

How often have you heard your customer say:

> "If only I could
> "I wish I ....
> "I'd love to ......
> "You just can't get ....
> "There's nowhere that sells..........

These are golden opportunities just waiting to be acted upon. What needs, wants and desires are presenting themselves to you? How can you build on your customer relationship by adding value for them? Positive words are also good to be on the lookout for as well, because if another face painter or entertainer is being praised and recommended by others for their service, you too need to be doing whatever it is that they're doing, and do it just as well or even better. Be on the ready to listen out for any negative statements as well that your customers may speak about such as "the face painter at the party last week never did this..." or "the entertainer was supposed to do that..." These words are signs of dissatisfaction from previous experiences – can you act on them and fill a gap in the market? How could you have made it better for them? If you're hearing the same problem time and time again there could be an unmet need out there. Maybe their needs are blocked in some way? Are there opportunities where your products or services can make a different impact into the market? Have new needs been created by changes going on around you, i.e., social, economical, cultural or technological. Can you capitalize on anything here?

Because we work in a fun-type of business it can be a bit difficult to think of a problem that the customer may actually be having, which can be a bit odd getting your head around. What you need to do is primarily think of the reasons why the person or company booked your services in the first place. Is it because they need you or want you. It could be for a number of reasons such as they had a very poor entertainer at their last event that didn't fully entertain the children to their expectations and had had complaints about it. Maybe they want to make a better impression this time round. Or could it be that they simply need to satisfy their daughters request to have you at her party from seeing you at the local school fete. From now on when a customer books you try to find out their reason for doing so – and start a list of 'reasons to book' going.

Do whatever you can to make your customers life easier by paying special attention to their needs, wants and desires and not just your achievement. Add some extra happiness, give them an amazing experience from just using your company, and by making them feel special you'll be surprised at how they'll view you and your business as you will certainly stand out from the rest. By having needs, wants and desires catered for, and customer problems solved - that in turn will lead to more customers seeking out your service. So listen out, and act as soon as you can. Is there something that your company can offer, can you help them in any way possible?

CHAPTER 6

Customer Care

Just How Good Is Your Customer Care?

Face painting at birthday parties and company events, although lots of fun and extremely lucrative, is not all about just providing your service for the fee being paid to you. How the booker perceives you and the support of the additional customer care that you provide will go a long way in building your image and your business model. It's all about going the extra mile and doing just a little bit more for each and every one of your existing customers and potential customers by providing a first-class service with additional unexpected things that your customer didn't expect that will put you way ahead of the competition.

Good customer care stems from how in-sync you are with the people who do business with you and those who use your service. Good customer care means that you are genuinely interested in serving them to your best ability and are always on the lookout on how you can make improvements.

Your number one priority in business is customer satisfaction. That's a priority. Unfortunately a lot of people in business view their customer as an interruption to work. I'm sure your know the sort of person I mean – they're the ones who tut-tut when you go into their shop and ask for advice right in the middle of when they're doing an important job like stacking the shelves or those who sigh loudly because you've interrupted them changing a light-bulb!! For goodness sake – without the customer who makes the business go round there wouldn't be a business to go round or the immortal light-bulb to change. Pause here for a moment and think about a recent time when you encountered appalling customer service from someone. How did that make you feel?

Another priority is how you handle customer's enquiries, a big area not to be pushed aside in our service industry. How do you follow-up with customers who phone or email you when you're unable to take their call for one reason or another? Make a decision and make it a discipline to follow up on every phone call, every lead and to answer every email that comes your way as soon as you possibly can. If you don't that will be a sure sign that you've become complacent in your business and your competitor will sense this and find a very quick path to the next company on their list.

Think of the times in the past when you've contacted someone and left an enquiry on their phone requesting to be phoned back, or you've been told that so-and-so will return your call shortly or there simply hasn't been any one on the end of the line to take your call. Can you remember how frustrated you felt as time slipped by and no return call; email or acknowledgement came your way. Because you want an answer NOW. How despondent you started to feel about the company or person you contacted because they couldn't be bothered to get in touch because you just weren't important enough, and how your mind starts to wander as you think of other ways to fulfil your needs, wants and desires as another competitor springs to mind. It can easily happen – you've been there before so don't make the same mistake of putting your customers through the same negative process. You need to do your utmost best to get back to all customer enquiries as soon as possible and show them that you are very much interested in them and their enquiry – after all, enquiries with no follow-up means no business.

Now I know some of you may be thinking 'Yeah but I work full-time so I can't physically get back to all enquires as they come in until I get home in the evening', well yes I understand this but I'm sure you have short breaks scheduled into your working day where it's possible to check your phone for any missed calls or messages. So in that situation where you have a few moments to spare it's then that you should quickly make an acknowledgement to any customer explaining that you're unable to answer their question in full at the moment and to let them know that they will hear from you as soon as you're available which will be in the next 10 minutes, 2 hours or at the end of the day (whichever it may be). This way your customer will know that you're on the ball and that you're not ignoring them and they'll be happy to wait to hear from you later. They will take satisfaction from the fact that you spared them a short moment of your time. In this fast-paced world that we live in with everyone wanting it NOW, needing it NOW and having answers to their questions NOW – I say Halleluiah for SmartPhones!!

One of the most effective areas of my business is by being totally disciplined every moment in time (where conceivably possible) to answer every email and text message as it comes into my phone, return every message placed on my landline as soon as I can and follow-up with all enquiries at the next available opportunity. Prospective customers like answers to their questions immediately, they like to be able to make a booking right now and they like to know that you care enough about them at this moment in time – they hate to have to wait around for you to get back to them, if you can be bothered to that is. An immediate response to a prospective customer or even a regular customer will enable you to be in the forefront of securing a booking before your competitors even have a chance to take breath, and because of this quick response strategy the customer is made to feel valued, you become highly regarded as a contentious service provider and before you know it the event is booked. I've had many instances where my prospective customer has returned back to me with comments such as 'Wow that was a fast response, thank you for replying so quickly'. It most definitely works as nine times out of ten I'm able to secure the booking.

Are You Going The Extra Mile

By being there for them when they need you will reassure your customer of your conscious ability and professionalism. You're there when they need you, there to answers questions and there to arrange an event with as soon as possible. This will have an overall reflection on the quality of the service that you provide in your face painting business as it will go a long way to enhance your business image, such as being punctual, thorough and considerate.

To go one step further in quality reassurance you could reinforce the conversation with the answers to their questions or notification of an event booked by sending them a brief email or text message outlining the details. Again this will accelerate the customer perception towards you as someone that is truly interested in them and actually takes the time to go the extra mile with exceptional customer care. Not only do you need to be as good as you possible can with providing your face painting activity, you need to be outstanding with your customer service as that will help to enhance your reputation and promote a good-feeling relationship with your customers. Excellent customer service is the cherry on the top of what you do.

Continually striving to improve on what you already do can be achieved by asking your best customer's one simple question, "What are we not providing that you would like us to". Listen very carefully on what they have to say and keep an open mind for gaps in the market and niche opportunities. Their answers may leave you feeling a bit taken aback and surprised but those answers will be a primary key in growing your business and building your customer relationship. The only opinion that matters is your customer's one. We aim to please. Is there something we're not offering you? What would you like us to provide. Tell us!

Casual conversations can in fact yield something constructive that you may have never discovered unless the conversation had taken place, and you may very well spot something that has been there all along. Discuss with your customers about what they liked about your company, what they didn't like, what they would like you to do differently and what new product or service they would like you to offer. This way you can probe for their un-met needs and desires and any queries that they may have in the general about the face painting and entertainment industry as a whole. During your time spent with them at their event, and if time and protocol allows, talk to them about any new service launches that are on the horizon and about any new trends that you have seen in the trade magazines, and whether or not it would be something that they may be interested in.

You can get your customers talking by leading them into conversation, but most importantly *listen* to what they have to say. Scrutinize your services regularly and keep asking yourself these important questions:

- What are my customers telling me?
- What are they saying that they want and need?
- What service or product would my customers buy today if I could have offered it to them?

- Are my customers satisfied?
- Are they loyal to me, and why are they loyal to me?
- Am I reaching my target market successfully?
- How can I improve my service to make it better than before?
- Is my service unique compared to the competition?
- Is my service level selling as I would expect it to?
- Can anyone copy my service and systems identically?
- Have I been presented with an opportunity today through a conversation with a customer or through something that I've seen?

Perfection will come over time as long as you continue to ask yourself the above questions and take action with all the answers.

Developing Ongoing Relationships

You may not know it yet but you are sitting on substantial potential that consists of the wealth that is hidden within the care and the relationships that can be built with your customers?

You know the old saying – "It's not what you know, it's who you know". Well that's all very well and good, but how about taking it one step further and thinking about – "It's *what you do* with who you know" – that really matters, and that will make all the difference.

By being genuinely interested in your customer is the beginning of the relationship that you should be building with them, and this relationship can last for many years, especially with B2B. The more someone likes you the better the relationship will become, and the more they trust you, the more likely they are to book your services or to buy your products again and again. Would you buy from a person that you didn't know, didn't like or didn't trust?

Listen closely when you are having a conversation with your customer and by this I don't mean just nodding or shaking your head in conversation and peering over her shoulder at what else is going on. Give good and interesting answers and comments. Make a mental note of anything they say that will help to build your relationship with them and be on the lookout for how you can provide a better experience.

So how can you stand out and be viewed as one of the best and most contentious face painters there is in your area? Let's look at a couple of ways that you can pull all the stops out.

- On arrival to an event give your customer a free gift, for no reason at all, just because you care. This could be a reward of some kind – maybe because she's the first customer this month or the first person to try out a new selection of face painting designs, or because it's a repeat booking. It's a nice idea to also gift wrap the items where possible using florists clear paper and curling ribbon to ensure an extra WOW factor.

Gifts that you could use include simple things for either the birthday child, party Mum or corporate booker, along the lines of:

A big bag of Pick 'n' Mix
Small colouring books and mini crayons
Bunch of birthday balloons
Party bags or Jamboree bags
Batch of freshly baked cupcakes
Crispy crème donuts with hot chocolate
Big block of Dairy Milk Chocolate
Mini bubble bath and body lotion
A seasonal pot plant
Flower hair clips for the girls
Plastic monsters or animals for the boys
Fairy dust packets or mini nail varnishes

When you dig deep and really think about it the list is endless of the low-cost gifts that you can offer as there are so many ways that you can make a good and lasting impression with additional customer care. By spending less than a fiver will go a long way to enhance your service provision.

- Really, really engage with the children you are working on especially the birthday child if it's at a private party. Make them feel so very special by talking to them as much as possible and engaging in conversation with them at their level. You should also go out of your way to engage fully with all other family members. Over the decades that I've been running Mimicks Face Painting

I've worked alongside many other allied entertainers and have seen those that have no enthusiasm or passion for the job they do and don't participate in any meaningful conversation with any of the children apart from their usual entertainment routine on which they are being paid for. Like I've said before – it's all about going the extra mile and adding more value to what you do as a standard practice.

• Make a mental note on anything they say to you that will help to build your relationship with them. Whatever the info is, write it down at your earliest convenience (could be a trip to the zoo, a holiday they've just had, or their child's tooth that's recently fallen out). You can them drop this into the conversation next time you see them. Your outstanding memory will go a long way and they'll be so impressed that you remembered such a trivial thing. A business owner with a good memory for personal information works a treat.

• Keep a diary to collect valuable customer information. When you're face painting at a party ask the birthday child what his favourite present was this year and then 6-weeks before his birthday next year send him a card and make a referral to the gift that he'd received. Mum will be flabbergasted that you remembered that information. We did this at Christmastime in our Grotto at Once Upon A Party – we remembered what present the child had asked Santa for and the following year we asked if he/she received it. The look on the parent's faces is priceless!

- On hearing or reading a story in the newspaper of something of interest about a customer of yours it's a great exercise to follow it up with an email or hand-written note to them to let them know that you saw the article and your specific comments relating to it. I saw an interview on one of my customer's children in our local paper that had participated in the Diabetes Fun Run and had raised a vast amount of money for the Charity. I immediately sent her a card to congratulate her on her endeavours. The Mum was well impressed that I'd actually taken the time and gone out of my way to send her a note congratulating her.

How have you been building relationships with your customers lately?

Customer Satisfaction Guaranteed

There are many different ways that you can probe into your customer's thoughts about what type of service they are looking for and what they are wanting from a face painter and a great way to find out is by using a Customer Satisfaction Survey on existing customers.

This survey can be done immediately after you have provided your service for them or it can be left with them to complete at their leisure after the service has taken place. It is always a good idea to enclose a pre-paid envelope for them to use if you would like them to post it back, however don't be too disappointed about the response rate as this can sometimes be quite low because they have to make the effort to go to the post-box.

Customer Satisfaction Surveys can be produced in all shapes and sizes from the ones where you would ask an open-ended questions and the customer would write an answer as a short comment, to the ones where you would ask a question that would have a Yes or No answer, to the ones where they score their satisfaction on a scale of 1:10 or on a scale between very satisfied to not at all satisfied. The comment based surveys will also double up as influential social proof and can be used as customer testimonials which we'll discuss in a later chapter.

Have a go at designing a Customer Satisfaction Survey and list questions like:

You and Your Company
• What they liked about you and your company
• Was the face painter's skill in application what was expected?
• Why they choose you as opposed to another service provider

Your Advertising and Sales Material
• Did an advert you placed play an important role in them booking
• Did they look at your website prior to making an appointment
• Did they book due to a special promotion being offered

The Service You Provided
- Was it value for money
- What did they like about the service you provided for them
- What did they dislike about the service you provided for them
- How likely would they be to re-book the same or similar event

The Appointment Process
- Were they satisfied with the booking process
- Was the date of their choice available
- Was the arrival to their event punctual by the face painting artiste

The After-Sales Process
- Were future needs discussed and advice given
- Was an opportunity for a future booking made

You could even produce a really simple survey by asking them to make comments on the four things that they liked about your service and the four things that they didn't like. This one works okay but most people feel too embarrassed about writing down their dislikes so tend to leave this box blank which doesn't help if you're trying to make improvements.

So get your thinking cap on and make a list of all the additional care that you can provide your customer with. Not only will your excellent customer care be pleasing to them, you will also get a great sense of satisfaction knowing that you have added value to their lives.

CHAPTER 7

Adding
Immense Value

Stop Selling and Start Giving

In business, as in life, giving is a great experience.

Generally small business owners are so wrapped up in how to increase sales and grow their business in order to improve their own lives that they forget and are missing one essential thing. How are they going to improve and add value to their prospects lives before they even become a customer, when they're a customer and after the service has been provided or product sold? They need to give, give, give and give more for free. We can become overly immersed in trying to find our next customer that we are missing the obvious point here. Start, and start today, thinking about making the life of your prospect easier before they book your service or purchase your product and they will be so surprised at how you are different from the masses that they will forever hold you in high esteem. It's a fantastic way of doing business knowing that you are making a big difference to people's lives before they actually part with their money.

We'll take a closer look at each of those three areas – before, during and after sales – and start with the value that we can provide to our customer even before they've signed on the dotted line.

Many years ago I was introduced to the giving strategy. I stopped selling to people and started giving to them long before they became customers, by adding value to *their* lives by giving them something that would be useful to them. Free reports on children's entertainment topics, free contact and resource lists for party planning, free 'How to Run A Stress Free Party' booklet. The list could go on and on. I sent them information in the post, I emailed them and I chatted to them on the phone. It's so true - the more you give the more you get.

The valuable lesson here is that most small business owner's only start giving to their customers after they have parted with their money. It, without a doubt, should be the other way round. You need to start giving to them well before they actually become your customer.

Can you imagine the look of surprise on your customers face when after an initial telephone enquiry that she made with you she then receives a special report by email on the must-have party foods that are really popular with kids. The free report you send out could include savoury snacks, scrummy desserts and a recipe to make a simple and effective birthday cake. This will be perceived as a welcome bundle of information that she can easily put to use immediately, whether she uses your services in the future or not.

When dealing with enquiries from potential customers you need to be thinking about how you can provide value to what they want? Devise some questions to ask and rehearse them until they are memorized. Always lead the customer by asking the right questions in the right order and of appropriate relevance. You must listen carefully to their answers and on this you can build your 'Value Adding' service from that. Focus on things that are of prime interest to the people you are trying to reach out to and in return make it your goal to help them fulfil their needs before they book you.

Some questions that you could ask a party customer looking to book you for their son or daughter's birthday party could be:

- Who else are they hiring for the party entertainment, if any, and would they like a list of all the entertainers in the area that you can recommend, such as clowns, magicians, DJ's and balloon modellers?

- Would they like you to point them to a great website that sells party ware, themed venue decor, party bags, favours and novelties?

- Would they like to receive a recipe for a delicious birthday cake?

- Would they like you to send them information relating to all the halls and community centres in their area along with their charges for party bookings and the all important telephone numbers and email addresses?

- Would they like a party time plan that outlines how to incorporate face painting into a two-hour event?

- A truly favourable one would be to ask if they'd like a list of party games which includes a running time plan for children's parties so that they're not left with the usual nightmare of "OMG I've run out of things to do and I still have 30 minutes left to entertain 20 out of control 5-year olds!

Even if they don't make a booking with you during their first point of contact, still offer them a bundle of free information and they'll certainly remember you and the value that you have added for them and you'll come to mind for their future events. Think about it, it's not costing you anything apart from some time in the beginning to make your reports that you can use time and time again, and that customer has useful information that you provided for free under no obligation to book your service that she will keep and use to remember you by next time. What a first-class service you are providing!

This is known as Adding Value which is all about going the extra mile and delivering more than the prospective customer expects. Consider ways of adding value to your services so that you have an edge over your competitors rather than just competing on price alone. This type of value adding free information can be tweaked to fit in with whatever type of enquiries you may be receiving for any of the services that you provide or the products that you sell – absolutely anything. You need think about everything it is that you offer to your customer and compile some sort of free information bundle that compliments the topic in question. This marketing strategy is a true win-win situation. They win with your free expertise and you'll win their trust.

Start to focus on the fact that the main purpose of your face painting business is to add value to the lives of the people that you come into contact with. Forget about making money and profits, forget about *you* and start thinking about *them* and what they want. Step into their shoes and do whatever it takes to help. Astonish them. Amaze them. Make them feel special. Give them something unanticipated. Cheer up their day. Send them a gift ..... anything that will let them know that you are different from other entertainers and that you genuinely care about them and their needs.

It's also wise to remember that if they don't buy from you this week that doesn't mean that they won't ever buy from you again. People's circumstances change week by week and month by month. Can you remember the leaflet that drops through your letterbox every six weeks from the local estate agent saying that they are short of homes to sell like yours, and to give them a call? I'll bet it goes straight into your waste bin, many, many times over . . . . until one day you decide to move home. Then that little leaflet and the estate agent becomes a service provider that you need to get in contact with immediately and possibly do business with. Everybody's buying situations change on a regular basis. You might not need it today, but someday in the future it may be just what you're looking for. The same scenario as explained above also applies to booking a holiday!

So here's my very strong suggestion to you. Take this concept and seriously think of ways that you can add value to the lives of your customers before they even do business with you. By differentiating yourself from the norm, you will be perceived in a different light, your reputation will soar and customers will then be seeking *you* out.

Fulfil their needs by adding additional and immense value to their lives.

Continue to Build a Value Adding Service

So your customer has booked your service and it's logged into your diary, you're pleased with yourself as another booking has been made. Now what. You do nothing more and just wait for the date to arrive? Surely not, as you can continue to build on this extra-ordinary relationship with this new customer by contacting them at least a couple of times more on the lead up to their event.

Telephone them and ask:

- Would they like you to arrive 30-minutes early to the event so that you can help them to set up and decorate, lay tables, help with the food at no extra charge?

- Would they like you to stay for an extra 30-minutes of stress-busting time after you've finished the face painting so that you can help with serving the birthday tea / washing up / playing games for no extra charge? Home-based parties for parents can sometimes be a bit fraught as they've generally got so many things to do in a short time-scale and may appreciate you giving a helping hand especially towards the end.

- Would they like you to provide any additional extras such as helium filled latex balloons, party bags, birthday cake, sweets and prizes? (these sorts of things can be detailed on your website).

- The day before the event send a courtesy text to say that you are looking forward to meeting them the next day and let them know your expected time of arrival and any requirements you may have, i.e. tables and chairs if applicable.

- If it's a birthday party you've been booked for, on the day of the party take along a personalised card for the birthday child. Maybe you can design your own cards showing different types of face painting designs. If Mum has told you before the party that her little boy wants to be a tiger, then give him a birthday card with a tiger face painting on it. You could even use this idea to send him a special little card six weeks before his birthday the following year with his painted face on it as a gentle reminder to book you again.

- Whilst at the party make a mental note of the birthday months of other children in the family along with their names (and write them down as soon as you get back in your car so you don't forget). You can then send an email to your customer prior to her other children's birthday dates and market yourself again. Maybe use the above strategy and send a card with their painted face on.

- The day after the event send a personalised hand-written thank you card to party customers and a headed letter to corporate bookers thanking them for choosing you as their service provider.

You have now built up the know, like and trust factor with your customer and a relationship of some sort has been started, even though it's just after only one booking.

Your business will grow so much faster as soon as you understand the importance of adding value to your customer's lives. Being in business is not, and should not, be all about making money! You should be filled with a burning desire by making it your goal to add some extra value so you will be perceived in a different light from the norm, and then you will feel an overwhelming sense of achievement knowing that you have truly served your customer in every sense of the word. If you are not doing well financially then you are not adding enough value to people's lives. Give your customers what they want and do it better than your competitors are doing it!

Your Follow-up System

Now moving onto the final step let's focus on the immense value that you are going to add after business has been done. You've done the groundwork by adding value to your customer's life before they buy and then you've provided your service for them. Then what? You stop in your tracks. You don't bother to telephone them, you don't bother to email them and you don't bother to write to them. Your customer feels abandoned. Shame on you - after such a good start. You see, business doesn't have to stop dead after the service has been supplied or the product has been sold. Far from it in fact. They may feel betrayed that they never hear from you again, that you've forgotten all about them as you haven't kept in contact with them!

You may be thinking to yourself "Well the service that I provide is only going to happen every so often so why bother to keep in touch". That's a very narrow-minded way of thinking as you'll have plenty of occasions to add value to the lives of existing customers. You need to be thinking of new things that you can offer to them, and just as important is to think about the things that you're not yet offering them. You only need to spend as little as an hour a month thinking about a one-off exclusive offer that you can market to your existing customer base. It doesn't take that long at all.

If someone has done business with you once they are far more likely to do business with you again. You've probably heard before that it's far easier and cheaper to do business with an existing customer than it is to go out and get a brand new one from scratch as they have built up the know, like and trust factor with you. Absolutely true. Without regular contact and follow-up with your existing customer base you'll lose that opportunity, and with your entire customer list combined you could stand to lose quite a bit of money. Your aim is to win your customers loyalty for life, to have them buying from you again and again and again, and that will only happen with a value-adding follow-up sequence. Your patience and persistence will pay off to a level that your competitors will not begin to be able to imagine and they are your fastest source to additional monthly profit.

So don't just do business and then ignore them. Send a regular newsletter which is always a great and easy way to stay in touch as the customer is still aware of your presence but under no pressure to make a booking or purchase a product. Don't forget that we're in the business of entertaining and there is so much information at our fingertips that we can put into a regular newsletter that can be sent to them. Just search the Internet for a specific topic and write about your findings and researches.

- Email them a monthly newsletter on things that are happening in the entertainment and events industry. There is plenty of information that you can source from trade magazines and the Internet. Even include research topics that aren't related to face painting like beauty tips, fashion trends and book reviews.

- Send out details of your refer and reward scheme that you operate, whereby if your customer refers you will reward her with a gift. More on that in another chapter.

- Send out a Costa Coffee voucher on Mother's Day to your best customers, or even a couple of cinema tickets. Give her something totally unexpected that is not connected to your business.

- Send out information on a children's colouring competition that you are holding on your website whereby the winner with the most creative picture will receive a £20 discount off a future birthday party event for any child in the family. Put the blank colouring sheets on your website for them to download and use – this way its gets them back onto your site.

- Send out details of homemade crafts for the kids to make at Easter, Halloween and Christmas. Include a blank face chart so that they can draw out their very own idea of a holiday themed face painting design.

- Send out a personalised hand-written Christmas Card.

- Share tips and reports by sending them to your Blog, Facebook page or Twitter account.

- Send them details of your latest service or product and let them know that as a valued customer they are privileged to be able to make a future booking with a 20% - 40% discount.

- Send out a personalised card to act as a gentle reminder about your face painting service for their pending party or event six to eight weeks prior to their next event taking place. Let them know that you enjoyed your time spent with them last year and if you can be of service to them again this year then they qualify for a special package.

The list is quite endless when you put your mind to it. Send anything that you can to add value to the life of your customer. It doesn't have to cost you the earth and generally it's just your time that you'll be spending – which you'll do once and send out to all your previous customers as once you have put these strategies in place they're so easy to roll out time and time again to everyone. Your follow-up system is important and must be utilized fully on each and every customer that has used your service before and it's a good idea to test a selection of sequences that you will be using. Most importantly, don't forget to put some sort of strap-line at the bottom of your mailing to promote you and your business (in a subtle and non-intrusive way of course) and a link that will lead them straight back onto your website.

There will of course be a handful of customers who don't want to hear from you again who will opt-out of your customer database, and this is quite the norm, so don't get upset or beat yourself up over it. Simply remove them from your list (or your autoresponder will automatically do it for you) and concentrate on those who are happy to hear from you. We'll also be going into more detail about email campaigns later on.

This is the time for you to think about and write down everything that you do now, as standard that adds value to the life of your customer that they are paying for. Then you can write down all the additional unpaid things that you do that adds value to the life of your customer, which in turn adds perceived value to you and your business. Are their many things that you already do? Next you can write down all the additional value-adding things that you're going to do for your customer starting from tomorrow and how you're going to implement your new strategies.

So next time, when a customer sings your praises, or when a recommendation comes in, or when you receive a letter of thanks in the post - you have done what you set out to do. You have added value to the life of your customer, which in turn has certainly added value to your ever-growing business.

CHAPTER 8

How Are You Selling Yourself?

Are You Promoting The Benefits?

The message that you need to get across should be all about letting your customer know about the benefits that your service or product will mean to them.

The 'benefits' of your business are how you make your customer feel, what it does to their self-esteem and the value that you are going to add for them. These are the benefits that need to be enforced into every paragraph of your advertising and your promotional material helping you to clearly stand out from the rest. The words that you write need to be all about what your customer needs and wants, well at least what you think they need and want. The words you write should not be all about you and what you've got. They are not interested in those features. What they do want to know about is how your service is going to benefit them, what experience it will bring and what you can actually do for them. You need to think about how you're going to massively improve their life when they do business with you.

Your prospective customer isn't interested in how brilliant you are, whether you are by far the best in town, how long you've been established, or what qualifications you hold. They're just not interested. They don't want to read all about you, you, you and your huge ego trip. These are your 'features' and quite bluntly no one really cares about them. Features are boring, uninteresting, and don't have enough information attached to them that will compel the prospective customer into making an informed decision about contacting you or not!

The features of your business which won't impress your customer are:

- Your length of time in the industry
- The brand of product you use
- Your low or high prices
- Your smart and impressive website
- Who your previous customers are
- The qualifications and experience you have
- The location of your business
- Your sign-written car/van that you drive

These are all features (and good ones I might add) of your business. Features should still be used however, but not as the main context of your sales material. People don't buy features, they don't care about your industry experience as it makes no odds to them – all they care about is the quality of the service that you will be providing to them and the experience that it will bring to the event.

Focus on the positive results of your service. People buy results. What is it that you're going to bring to them, what is the benefit of using you, what is the experience that they will have? Focus on your advantages. What problems do you solve? If you surf through the Internet you will probably see that most face painters and children's entertainers are all hammering home their features, me, me, me, me!

You'll find that typical paper-based advertising the sort that you see in newspapers and community magazines from an extensive array of businesses usually go along the lines of: their logo, followed by a feature, followed by bullet points with more of their features, followed with their telephone number and address. Where are the benefits to the customer?

Try this out for a little exercise. Go and get a local magazine, Yellow Pages or newspaper and thumb through the pages looking at all the adverts placed there. What do you see? Plenty of features I expect. I took a look through our community magazine that dropped on the doormat this month and it was filled with things like:

- Painter & Decorator – All Interior Work Undertaken.
- Cleaning Services – Domestic Cleaning and Office Cleaning.
- Building Services – Free Estimates and Advice. No Obligation.
- Bouncy Castle Hire – Established in 2004.

- School of Motoring – Fully Qualified Instructor.
- Pet Surgery – Friendly Family Run Business.
- Hair Salon – Professional Cutting and Colouring Specialists.
- Beauty Salon – listing every conceivable qualification.

And the list could go on and on. Boring, uninteresting and not compelling enough for the customer to pick up the phone because it's not saying what's in it for them, they're only listing features, me, me, me, me, me. Those were the main taglines for those companies. What value do they offer their customer or client? None whatsoever. Not one of them is selling the benefit, the end result. Instead they are all selling themselves and their ego.

What reason from the list above is given for the customer to contact the service provider – none whatsoever. They want to know how you're going to make a difference, they want to know what value you are going to give to them and what problem or need of theirs you are going to solve for them.

Remember benefits first – features later.

Getting The Message Across

As an example let's look at the service we provide. The feature of face painting is in the name . . . its Face Painting. But the benefit of the face painting is how it's going to make your customer feel and look. It's the emotional experience that is attached to the face painting which is the benefit, and it's that which must be promoted in order to sell it. That's what the customer is buying – the end result and not the name of the service provided. This also applies for Glitter Tattoos, Henna Bodyart and Hair Braiding.

Stating the benefits of your face painting business is what you should be concentrating on when writing the copy for your adverts, the copy for your sales literature, your website and your business cards. In fact anywhere and everywhere that your customer sees your written words should have the emphasis focused on the benefits to them.

Here are a few pointers in the right direction of what a benefit is and how you could include them in your advertising and marketing:

- How is your service going to make your customer feel – a benefit
- How is your service going to make your customer look – a benefit
- What need of theirs will you be fulfilling – a benefit
- What is it going to do to their self-esteem – a benefit
- What added value are you going to bring – a benefit
- What is the final result that you are selling –a benefit
- What incentive to book now are you offering – a benefit

You need to stop thinking features, or how brilliant you are, or how good your service or product is, as the customer will judge that for themselves. Instead start to fixate on your customers mind and about the benefits that you will bring to them through experiencing your service or product. Sell the emotion, the outcome, the final result of your service, and sell how it will make the customer feel by booking you.

Put this into practice when you next place an advert, or design a brand new leaflet or are writing copy for your website. What does your message say to your potential customer? Your advert must sell the benefits of the end result and not just the features of your service.

Selling The End Result

So how do you sell the end result? You need to take a step back and think about what your service provides as an end result and what problem does it solve? Your customer is buying the end result so the final outcome of your service is what you should sell. Make sure that all your literature reflects the end result – the benefits.

Let's take some general everyday scenarios here:

- When you book an appointment at a hair salon you don't see the trendy surroundings, the immaculate staff uniform and the adequate parking facilities. Features. What you imagine is your beautiful shining and conditioned hair, a fantastic cut that is the best you've ever had and how you will feel knowing you look absolutely fabulous. You see the end result and the pleasure that it will bring. The benefit.

- When you book a mobile nail technician you don't see her expensive kit box or marvel at her state-of-the-art UV curing lamp. Features. What you do see is your stumpy short nails and ragged cuticles transformed into perfectly extended talons with its stunning polish or nail art. You see the end result – the benefit.

- When you buy a joint of meat you don't just see the meat in its plastic wrapper. Instead you imagine the roast dinner with delicious potatoes and vegetables and perhaps you even see the table setting in your mind's eye. So gone is the vision of a piece of cold meat sitting tightly on a polystyrene tray wrapped in film, and in its place you can see a lovely dining experience, perhaps with friends. The benefit.

- When your front lawn is in dire need of attention, you don't care what special chemicals will be used, you don't care how long the gardener has been in business and you certainly don't care what van he'll be driving. What you imagine is a beautiful lush lawn that is short, well trimmed and very green. You might even see the look of envy on your neighbour's faces! The benefit.

Are you getting the picture here? In everywhere that you are using words, whether written or spoken, it is a skill to master the ability to write or speak good copy that sells. People think in pictures so provide an image to be placed in your customers mind. I expect that images came to mind for you when you read all the above scenarios didn't they? How well do you think you are scoring with your copy writing? Is your customer seeing the picture? Are you selling the end result or purely the name of your service? If it's the latter you need to stop selling face painting and start selling the end result, start selling the emotion, start solving the customer's problem and start selling the value.

Now, go through your own adverts and literature (leaflets, etc) and take a long hard and critical look at your copy writing. What benefits to the customer are you promoting? Be honest with yourself – is there room for improvement? If so, start now. Start writing effective copy that tempts your customers into doing business with you!

CHAPTER 9

Setting Your Prices

Are You Being Paid What You Deserve?

What if you realised that everything you thought you knew about setting your prices was wrong. Setting prices for your service is such a challenging task and for many small business owners the big question is how do you get it just right? How do you come up with the best price that the customer will be happy to pay, with the best profit margins for your face painting venture?

Your pricing structure is extremely important as you really need to get it right from the onset. If you charge an unbelievably high price for your services you will price yourself out of the market, and if you drastically undercut and price way too cheaply you'll become a threat to your competitors and run the risk of bad feelings between you and them. Do your market research thoroughly at this stage and gain as much information about your competitors pricing structures as possible and try to keep the consistency of similar prices going. You will need to take into consideration however their quality of service, their reputation in the industry, their longevity of practice and their comparable qualities to you and your business.

There are a couple of pricing strategies that I would like to share with you, but first I must make it clear that what is right for one face painter may not necessarily be the best for another due to many influential circumstances such as location, experience and nerve!

Have a look at the three different pricing strategies below and see which one your face painting business fits into:

1. **Do you feel compelled to put your price in line with your competitor?**

   Are you setting your prices to match the competitors in your area? Is this the right thing for you to do? Is this the best market price for the best value? Where did they get their pricing strategy from anyway? Did they just pluck this figure from thin air? Is their service superior or inferior to yours? Do you have the same skill-set and are they faster or slower in their service than you? Does their business have the same over-heads and advertising expenses? Do they have staff to pay, or a commercial car or van to run? Are they working the business as a part-time pocket money hobby or as a full-time business? And finally – why do you compare yourself to your competitor?

2. Do you feel that you should lower your price to get more business?

Maybe to win more business you have decided to lower your prices to beat your competition. Lowering your prices is by far the worst thing you can do, if you do that then you are in fact 'buying your work'. This is going to do nothing for the way your customer perceives you as you will very fast become known as cheap, poor quality, and amateurish. You're also making it hard for everyone else by de-valuing the industry as a whole. You'll eventually be in a situation where you'll find it almost impossible to increase your prices overtime as a precedent would have been set by you. Is that what you have gone into business for, to offer your skill and services for a cheap price? You must remember that you are not a Charity – you're in business and should be paid for the value that you are going to bring to the party or event. If the customer wants a budget price then she can go seek an alternative source, maybe using Auntie Sarah who'll have a go face painting with a mediocre set of face paints from China that clearly states on the box 'not to be used around the eyes or mouth'! Even in this economic downturn, lowering your prices will be the worst thing you can possibly do.

3. Do you charge over and above the normal rate?

Are you brave enough to charge over and above the industry norm? Are you a first-class face painter with an elite skill? Great, then charge for it. Don't devalue yourself; ask for what you deserve to be paid and be recognized for the value that you are adding to your customer's lives. It's a big mistake to believe that you can't increase your prices, especially in a bad economic climate. A total myth. Don't under-sell yourself. A word of warning here though – you'll be run out of town if you charge high fees for just a bog-standard service. You must be exceptional in what you do, willing to go the extra mile by adding immense value to the lives of your customers, then indeed you can charge the high fees you so rightly deserve!

So looking back at the three different pricing strategies, which one do you fall into within your face painting business? Are you content with where you are now? We are positioned quite comfortably in position number three and provide our customers with a first-class service every time.

As competition in our industry has grown immensely I often hear about face painters, not necessarily in my area, charging ridiculously low prices for a birthday party. I even heard of one lady charging £1 per face. That's not a business; it's a hobby (and a cheek). Those who charge very, very low fees really need to wake up and smell the coffee and divide the income between the labour time involved, the getting ready time involved, the getting to the party time involved, the cleaning of the kit when getting home time involved, let alone the fuel, the insurance, the administration costs, etc, etc, etc. You never hear of a clown or a magician doing a two-hour party for £20. De-valuation and poor price indications will have a moral knock-on effect.

You may feel like you're in a catch-22 situation when you first start up as a face painter as you realise that you've got a long way to go with regards to skill and speed. You'll probably feel the urge to charge a fairly low price in the beginning just to get yourself out there as you may not feel confident in charging what other face painters are. Big mistake unless you don't have any intentions of running this new enterprise of yours as a business, and are just going down the hobby route! When you calculate all the costs involved which includes preparation before the party and kit maintenance after the party, fuel (45p per mile at the moment) and travel time, your labour charge for when you are providing your service and your product costs, all these things will add up. Most often a one-hour event will actually take three hours of your time as it's all of the logistics combined. If you divide a low-fee that you may be charging by the three hours, at the end of the day is it actually worth it? Stacking shelves in a supermarket would be financially better and you wouldn't have the stress-factor of running a business to contend with either!

There are, however, customers out there who will only buy on price alone and not on quality and you'll find that 'budget' is their middle name. Maybe you know someone like that, always looking for a cheap bargain or a massive discount, or maybe complaining about a service in order to get the price down! However, it's also worth remembering that there are people out there who will always pay that little bit extra for value, for the experience it brings, and for the self-esteem it bestows. They will buy the perceived value. These customers can afford it; in fact 5-10% of your existing customers can afford it – so go the extra mile and add-on an extra element, maybe an up-sell to your service that is different to what you sell to the majority. You will always have customers who are willing to pay for an elite version of what you do at a far higher price.

As you can see from the list below there will always be those people who will pay extra for value, experience and for their own self-esteem, which includes:

- Those who travel first-class – it's the same train or plane that transports the people to their destination and it gets them all there at the same time, but there will always be those who will pay to be more comfortable, and to feel more valued than the rest and for a better experience.

- Those who will pay a considerable sum extra for the senior professional stylist in a top-notch hair salon as opposed to the trainee working in the chair next to her.

- There will always be those who dress themselves and their family in designer clothes and wouldn't dream of anything less.

- There will always be those who patron the most expensive and lavish restaurants and wouldn't be seen in a fast-food outlet.

- Those who will pay extra to enhance their image and self-esteem and that of their children's by being the first to choose something that is the best, is new, different, unique and unusual - keeping up with the Joneses' so to speak.

Think about your buying behaviour as well. What do you pay extra for to provide you with extra value for money? Do you firstly decide what you want to buy and then go and look for it, or do you decide on the price to spend and then go looking for the item to fit the cost (this is buying on price alone and taking nothing else into consideration). Think about it and make a list of your 'price no option' purchases. Shoes and handbags might be one of yours – it certainly isn't one of mine!

Incidentally, I must also point out that no-one should ever have the right to haggle about your prices as they are instantly de-valuing you and your skill that you've worked hard to achieve. If someone asks you for a discount, say 10%, you could try the answer "Yeah sure. So what 10% shall I take off my service for you – maybe miss out 10% of the children to be painted". It gives you the upper hand and works every time. It's a fabulous remark, and my husband even uses it in his double-glazing business - "Yeah sure I can cut the costs, he says, so which window shall I leave the glass out of?"!!!

How Do You Put Your Prices Up?

You may worry about putting your service price up to reflect your true value, and I totally understand where you're coming from. It's a sort of mental-barrier and at the same time a no-brainer. You want and need to put your prices up but you worry that business will not be as brisk and might take a downturn. I must admit I did have that mind-set for many years until I was introduced to the 'Putting Your Prices Up Formula' that I'm about to share with you.

Let's do some sums here to see how it adds up:

- Let's say you charge an industry-average price and convert 90% of your customer enquires (let's say 9 out of 10 make a booking with you) at £100 per 3-hour event.

- This will bring in revenue of £900 for 9 events - over 27 hours of service time.

- Now put your price up to £130 per 3-hour event. You may lose 20% of business enquiries here and it will give you a 70% ratio (7 out of 10 make a booking with you).

- The great thing here is that this higher price will bring in revenue of £910 for 7 events over a 21 hour time-span. So therefore it works out to be more money in the bank for fewer bookings provided and for fewer hours worked!

So as you can see, by putting your price up you can actually make more money than before and you'll spend less time earning it. This is working SMART as compared to working HARD. I tried this system many, many years ago and had to actually put my prices up three times (yes three times) before I noticed a drop in bookings, but I still earned more money for less input. Think about the enquiries that you get and then try to come up with your approximate number of how many you convert to customers. If you convert 100% of enquiries then you're way too cheap! I reckon it could be time to put your prices up. Make it a condition to test this process starting next week by choosing a price increase that you are comfortable with. Give it a go for one month and you could be nicely surprised by your results, as long as you are sure of your previous conversion ratio. Rejoice in the results and untapped profits that could lie before you.

Let's recap - never think about lowering your prices, instead think about how you can get more by adding extra value to your service that you are providing. Add on a bonus product or service to what you already offer giving your customer an incentive to book you. So go on, give it a try – add something of better value to what you already do, and then aggressively market it to your customers. You'll find that there will be willing purchasers of your elite/bespoke service and you wouldn't want to miss out on that 5-10% of customers who are willing to pay more for a superior version of what you do.

Heard It All Before

If you've been face painting for a while and attended the usual school fete, village fun day, country show or festival, you will be well aware of what I am about to say. I'd just like finish this chapter with the two most common, yet contradicting and annoying statements you have probably heard time and time again – which go like this:

"She must be raking it in"

- A usual remark by someone watching you who is envious and feels that they can do what you're doing just as easily and that it's money for old rope. Huh – if only they knew.

"You can't make money out of Face Painting"

- A remark often heard from those who have given it a go, with no commitment to marketing or promoting themselves, who just expect the bookings to come rolling in so they can earn a fortune without any effort on their part.

Yep, we've heard it all before!

CHAPTER 10

How To Write A Business Plan

Your Road Map to Success

Your self-employed business life is going to be very hectic and even more so if you also have the commitment of another job, or are bringing up a family. There will be telephone calls to make, letters to write, advertising to plan and client databases to build – let alone the day-to-day emergencies, which will pop up quite frequently sapping your valuable time. It's all going to take a lot of hard work and total dedication.

Short-term issues should not divert you from your long-term goals and crucial business planning. Writing a business plan is not as daunting as you may first think, you are merely encapsulating your objectives and writing them down such as what you intend to achieve and what resources you'll need. Think of it a bit like going on a long journey from say Southampton to Manchester. What do you intend to achieve from the journey (to get from Southampton to Manchester) and what resources will you need to accomplish that (a car, some sort of road map, fuel, road tax and a drink and packet of sandwiches maybe).

So what type of plans are needed? Well basically there are three.

1. An Objective Master Plan
2. A Cash Flow Plan.
3. A Business Finance Plan

Let's take a look at each one individually.

The Objective Master Plan

Do you actually know where you're going in your face painting business today, next month or even next year? Is that information logged somewhere? Do you have a written master plan for your future success or do you just have hopes and dreams floating around in your head? A lot of self-employed people just hope for the best without giving a second thought to a plan of action for creating the type of business they'd be happy with. They've become conditioned into having a wishbone rather than a backbone, as the saying goes. Unfortunately, a very big mistake.

There are so many supporting reasons for writing an objective master plan as you embark on your future, which is an important aspect in the creation of a successful business. Without one in place that lists exactly what you hope to achieve and accomplish, it's highly unlikely that you'll succeed let alone reach your desired fortune if it's all just pie in the sky.

Your objective plan will be filled with all your exciting hopes, ideas and aspirations for your growing face painting business and it will always serve as inspiration to you. There is nothing quite like writing down your forecasts on paper and over the coming years watching them happen. Your objective master plan should also include other personal aspects of your life as well and not only be written about your business ones. Embrace these other areas and include things such as family, relationships, holidays, material things and anything else you should desire. It will be all about putting the pieces together making them fit into your work and life puzzle, allowing them to harmonise together. Think of your plan as an aspiration for the life that you want and then create it over a three-year time-span (long-term goals), broken down into twelve monthly segments (short-term goals).

One point to remember here is that in business there is never a straight path that can be followed. We tend to get from A to B and then from B to C in a sort of wiggly wobbly fashion – known as diversion. Slight diversification off the straight and narrow is totally acceptable as long as you are always focused on the end result, whether that's a short-term goal or a long-term goal, and get yourself back on track.

Even though you will be setting a forward thinking plan, it's not set in stone as things will happen beyond your control, your desires and priorities will change and your experience will grow. The important point is to write your plan for the future in today's context as if you had already achieved the goals that are listed, given your current abilities. Your plan will become a source of stimulation to you over the coming months as you read and re-read them.

To write in today's context you'd put something like: "During this year I will double my customer list and I will put one new marketing activity in place each and every week. I'll have a website up and running by the fourth month and I will have designed a new brochure by month five. In month seven my Face book page will be up and running and will be getting twenty new Likes each week. My family and I will take a two-week holiday in the spring and a short weekend break in the autumn".

An easy trap to fall into is that of starting out in business, fulfilling a couple of steps on your objective master plan and then running out of time and motivation. If you're hesitant about guiding your business through efficiently to its profitability stage, then you may be better off not even writing a plan!

Anyone can go into business expecting to earn a fortune, but if they don't have plans, actions and goals outlining their road-map to success – how on earth are they going to get there and reach their desired destiny. By putting pen to paper and actually writing your plans down will help you to understand what it is that you want to achieve over a certain time-span from your face painting business and will allow you to put in motion the activities that will help you to get there. It really is as easy as that. Your objective master plan will be your road-map to success for without one, you won't get very far.

Once your objective master plan has been written it shouldn't be stuffed away in a draw somewhere out of sight. It should be close to hand and used as an inspiration tool – or you could say a kick up the butt! By checking your plan on a monthly basis will keep you on the right track and you'll be able to clarify whether your business growth is indeed progressing at the right pace. Your vision must be one that will literally pull you into the future, will scare you a little bit and make your heart beat a little faster than normal whenever you read it. Make you aspirations very specific, measurable, and realistic and at the same time a bit of a stretch.

The Cash Flow Plan

When you plan a day of retail therapy you generally write yourself a shopping list, or you may just store it in your mind. This list could include new jeans, jumper, shoes, a CD, and some luxury smellies for the bathroom. You stuff a £20 note into your purse and off you go on your journey. Come the end of the day you are going to be left feeling really despondent and unenthused, as your twenty pounds didn't stretch as far as you hoped it would. You just didn't have enough cash to buy everything you needed and wanted that was on your list!

A cash flow plan is no different and is very much tied into your objective master plan. You know what you want, but have you got the available funds to get it? You need to be able to forecast the flow of cash that you have available – thus a cash flow plan.

You can write your cash flow forecast on a month by month scale:

- Plan a forecast of the money you anticipate coming into your business - services rendered, invoices rendered, products sold, miscellaneous income, and any capital you may invest. Simply put it means making a list of all the money you expect to earn on a realistic scale and try not to over-exaggerate here. This is the cash flow coming in.

- Plan a forecast of the money you will need to pay out to suppliers for purchases, wages to yourself (drawings), any tax due, marketing and advertising costs, telephone bill, fuel costs, professional fees, general expenses, bank charges, insurance and any other expenses.

It's very important to make realistic assumptions here and to try and account for every eventuality, which is sometimes easier said than done!

By keeping your cash flow forecast in line with your bank account will help to throw up any situations when your need for cash is at its greatest. For example in the leaner winter months when you may find that business is slower than usual, you'll be able to plan your cash accordingly to meet pending payments and expenses. Those lean months that will flag up from time to time may not be the time to invest in training, or to expand into a new product range or to kit yourself out with a new uniform. Don't forget that most businesses fit into the feast and feminine category, and our face painting industry more-so than others as it's very seasonal.

Once you have your objective and cash flow plans written you'll be able to work out your personal survival budget and what you would like to earn from your business. An easy way to do this is to calculate your turnover from the past three months (this is the money you received for services rendered) and then take away all your expenses, excluding personal drawings. This amount can now be divided between three months and this will give you your average monthly income, and then divide by four will give you your average weekly income. From this income figure you would then work out what you would like to earn, or can afford to earn on a weekly basis. If there is any money left in the pot after all the expenses have been paid and accounted for, is your business profit.

By doing this exercise regularly over three months, six months and a year will enable you to understand the viability of your business.

You will then be able to ask yourself the following questions:

- Is there sufficient turnover in my business?
- Am I earning enough in wages to meet my needs?
- Do I need to look at my pricing structures and improve them to increase my turnover?
- Do I need to add a new service or product to generate extra income?

Taking time to track the progress of your turnover will throw some light onto how your business is moving forward and growing. Ideally you need to see a situation whereby each quarter the business has improved on the last quarter, even if it's only a slight difference, and then by checking it on a year to year basis. By the time you have been in business for a couple of years you will be prepared for those impending lean months that you know will be looming (we all have them) so that you can plan your cash flow accordingly and also look forward with anticipation to those forthcoming fruitful months – the famine and the feast.

The Business Finance Plan

This is a more thorough and comprehensive plan than the two above, and its intended use is for financial backing from a bank or investor.

This plan combines your objective master plan and your cash flow plan but on a 'no fail' basis. It must be thorough and conservative regarding the future of the business along with projected sales and costs, especially if you are handing it over to a bank manager or a financial investor.

If you do need financial backing for the future and growth of your business, your financial backer will need instilled confidence in you and your judgement. However, your business finance plan must achieve a balance between optimism and realism in order to persuade those that you are seeking either a bank loan or a business investment.

So what will you need to put into your business finance plan? Here are a few necessary elements:

- What is the business – this will be a brief overview including when it was started, what is its nature, what has been its previous trading history.

- The management structure – who you are and what's your previous employment and qualification history, what are your strengths and weaknesses in management, and how you will recruit if additional staff is required.

- The service and/or product – a simple description of what you offer and your pricing structure and how it will be developed over time to meet current trends.

- Who is your customer – who is your target market that your service and/or product is aimed at, how often do they buy.

- How will you market your business – compile a list of all your proposed marketing strategies?

- Who is your competition – their size and position in the marketplace, what are their strengths and what are their weaknesses.

- What is the potential for business growth – over a five-year time span?

- How much investment or loan is required from the bank or lender – and how you will pay it back, and what is your exit strategy if the business fails.

- A full financial analysis of the forecasted profits for the next three-years.

As you can see from above the business finance plan is quite heavy going and is not something that can be put together on a tea-break. This plan will need thorough research and will need to be presented in a professional manner prior to submitting to any finance lender.

Your objective, cash flow and finance business plan shouldn't be written and then forgotten about. They should be used as a reference and progression tool for your business. By returning to them on a regular basis will enable you to make changes for the better, it will highlight any areas that you may feel need your immediate attention to avoid a spiralling downturn, and will provide enthusiasm and inspiration to push your business onto its next level of growth.

Remember the saying – 'If you fail to plan you'll plan to fail'.

Once you get going you'll build up a momentum with your business planning and things should go from good to great. By making sure that you have the above strategies in place from the onset will all help to make your business run as a smooth operation.

CHAPTER 11

Marketing Your Business

Get Yourself Out There Big Time

Marketing – quite a scary word, don't you think?

The very mere thought of marketing your face painting business can give you brain frieze, just like when you eat your favourite ice cream – pleasure from the results but it can be a very painful experience getting there! For some, the thought of how to successfully market their business can turn their legs to jelly and put a knot in their stomach. Maybe you're one of those reluctant marketers too, worrying about what others may think of you. If so, you need to reframe how you view your marketing strategies because if you're in business then your customers need you and they need to know how to get hold of you. Remember that you do the job you do, to help others and to effectively solve their problems.

Mimicks Face Painting has been using many profitable marketing tactics for many years now and this section of the book is dedicated to revealing the success stories, the tactics and the systems that made us successful in every way possible. I've learned and developed some sound concepts and special techniques that are easily transferable from my business straight into yours and hopefully I'm going to shine a brighter light for you to follow in all your marketing endeavours. There are many sources of marketing out there that you could use, and whether you choose to take and put into practice the information that I can provide for you, or you choose another source of provider – the bottom line is - *are you going to make it happen?* So over the next few chapters we'll take a look at how to make your inspirational ideas really stick, and turn your fears of marketing into the supporting success story of *your* face painting business, which will leave your competitors still standing in the ice-cream queue!

If you want to attract more customers so that they can book your face painting service – then those customers need to know that you're out there waiting for their business. You need to get yourself 'out there' by actively marketing your business, big time. Big time!

Firstly you need to remember that providing your service is not the priority in your business as it's all about the marketing of your service, which is your fastest way to wealth. So stop being just a face painter and become the marketer of your face painting business as well. That's the big difference between earning just enough pocket-money to get by to actually earning substantial sums from your venture. You need to put as much focus into your marketing plan in order to get more customers to experience what you do rather than spending all your energy on just doing face painting. So put your paints down and stop playing around with them and concentrate ON where the money is coming from – it's certainly not coming from painting practice on your arm or leg.

If you change your mindset and start to work ON your business rather than IN your business by introducing new marketing systems and seeing them through then your business growth will soar. I have built up many of my businesses by using this strategy – in the beginning I was always the chief cook and bottle washer, and over time employees were hired to lessen my load, and with my load lessened the businesses grew as I was able to commit more time *on* the business. I was able to put plans into action and I was able to accomplish new ideas and implement new services or bring in new retail products. Soon it could be time for you to hand over the tools of the trade for some of your events to someone else (even if in the beginning it was only a few parties here and there) and time for you to take control of the reigns and push your business in the direction of success with a sound marketing plan. Remember - it's not all about doing your thing, it's all about marketing your thing!

Marketing is Like Gardening

Before we get going with this chapter you need to remember that Marketing is the same as Gardening:

- In gardening you plant a seed with expectations of growth. In marketing you plan a strategy to implement with expectations of growth.

- In gardening you water that seed to promote growth and in marketing you keep adding more ideas into the mix to promote growth.

- In gardening you remove some shoots to help the plant expand and develop further. In marketing you remove a few ineffective tactics in order to concentrate on the more effective ones.

- In gardening there comes a time when that baby plant needs to be re-potted because it's outgrown its original one, so you find a bigger pot. In marketing those first initial small ideas you once had are growing very successfully so you now need to expand with your software, design a bigger and better website or move into the larger and more profitable shows and festivals.

- Your baby seedling has now turned into a magnificent plant through the love and care that you enriched it with. It gives you much pleasure knowing that you gave it life and the people who see it admire your skill and expertise. Your business has grown from that initial thought into an outstanding company and you feel very proud of your endeavours and your customers hold you in high-regard because they know that you care about them.

- In gardening if you don't continue to feed and water your plant it will stop blossoming, it will become dehydrated, crinkle up and it will die. That's your fault. Not the environments fault, the economy's fault, your partners fault or the plants fault. It's your fault, because you just didn't care enough. In marketing if you don't continue to nurture your ideas, implement your strategies, build customer relationships, expand your business principles, look for opportunities to exploit, promote yourself with a vengeance – well in a nut-shell your business will die. That's your fault. Not the environments fault, the economy's fault, the banks fault, your competitors fault, the industry's fault. It's your fault, because you just didn't care enough. People with unsuccessful businesses are always so quick to blame other people and other situations for their downfall, they never once stop to think to themselves 'Well maybe it's my fault that my business collapsed'!

So as you can see marketing is so like gardening – when things are looking good it's all because you have made it possible, and made it happen and when things are looking bad it's a reflection of your actions, or lack of actions that caused the whole thing to shrivel up and die! Go and buy a pack of plant seeds and you'll see what I mean.

Secret Services and Private Products

If you've got the expertise, the talent and the goods that people want and need but have little or no self-promotion, how are your potential customers going to find out about you? It's your duty as a small business owner to get out there and promote your services or product to as many people as you can or else you run the risk of depriving someone of your solution to their problem! If your intention in business is to be successful, and I'm absolutely sure it is - you need to be drawn towards that main sense of purpose. Having energy and determination with your marketing, how you connect with new customers or reconnect with existing ones, is a necessity for your future accomplishment.

You're in business, so remember to show off. Think of your business as an extension of who you. You should be strutting your stuff and blowing your own trumpet, as loud as you possibly can, as you'll do yourself no favours by having a secret service or a private product (what's the point of that). Get out there and market yourself to the masses because unfortunately no-one else is going to do it for you.

A lot of small business owners hate the thought of self-promotion in the fear of being too pushy and too 'in ya face' when it comes to marketing, as any rejections they incur could be felt on a personal level. How many times have you walked past someone doing market research in the street and you've said "No thank you" to them when they try to encourage you to stop. They get rejection after rejection after rejection, but they still keep going with a smile on their face. They know that they'll have to hear those formidable words 'No thank you' many, many times before they will manage to hook someone who is willing to stop and give them their time and say 'Yes'. The same thing will apply to your business marketing as you'll need to be persistent, you'll need to be alert and you'll most certainly need to feel confident in your self-promotion because eventually someone will say yes to your phone call, or your advert or your mail-shot. So don't hide away in the dark and expect your customers to find you, because they won't. If you want more business, you have to go after it at full force.

Struggling business owners who are feeling the pinch and just about making ends meet will glaze over when they hear the word marketing. They're the ones who tend to carry on as they always have, getting what they've always got – which will inevitably be a struggling business. You know the old saying "If you always do what you've always done, you'll always get what you've always got". I'll repeat that – If you always do what you've always done, you'll always get what you've always got. I hear face painters complaining about how slow business is, and not many bookings lined up, and when I ask how they are promoting themselves they say "Oh just the usual way of handing out leaflets at school fetes and birthday parties"!!! They're standing still and not moving the business forward to a higher level by becoming *outstanding* in their marketing. A handful of leaflets here and there are not going to make a thriving business. Successful business owners on the other-hand will light up when they hear the word marketing as they understand its purpose and its importance for creating wealth and putting money in the bank. Unfortunately, without marketing in any shape or form, your business ain't going nowhere sunshine!

Remember earlier I explained to you that your number one priority in your business is in getting customers and secondly it's doing the actual face painting. Well as much as you love being out there doing your thing, soaking up all the positive comments of admiration for your work and your talent, and feeling really good about how happy you have just made your customer, you need to put just as much creative energy (if not more) into the advertising, promotion and marketing of your business in order to get more customers.

By making a decision and laying down a discipline and agreeing to yourself that **once a week** you will endeavour to do **one marketing activity** within your business that in turn will make money, will be a huge step in the right direction. There are so many different ways that you can sell your service or promote your product to potential customers and if you're spending time on a daily basis to practice your face painting skills you'll need to put the same amount of conviction and passion into developing at least one new marketing activity each week, yes one new one each week.

When putting your marketing plan into action it's imperative to take into account the specific holidays and seasons taking place throughout the year, and never miss an opportunity to promote something that fits well with the theme to entice your customers. These types of events can creep up on you and before you know it and its School Fete

SHERRILL CHURCH | Mimicks Face Painting

Time or Christmas Party Time – so plan well in advance and start contacting or promoting to potential bookers well in advance. I have a dedicated yearly wall planner that details all the seasonal events that will be taking place and some three-months in advance I contact the relevant bookers to promote my service. You also need to be adding your seasonal promotions to all your sales material and internet marketing.

Barriers to success are usually due to indecision to make your business successful. A case of "Ahh now what shall I do first – this or that?" If you can't make decisions, no-one's going to do it for you. So don't be a ditherer. The minute you start your face painting business, that's the minute you need to start marketing it. You can't spend all your available time just doing the face painting service provision, or at worse spending valuable time with painting practice on your own arm – you've got to promote yourself in every way possible. Decide on your marketing strategy and just get on with it.

So where to start – well here's a little helping hand of some of the procedures that you could be using, which I'll be going through in more detail soon.

You'll need to get yourself a good marketing mix that should include some, if not all of the following:

1. **Advertising:** What are you already doing? Scrutinise it. Are you doing influential direct response adverts with grabbing headlines and persuasive call to actions which produce clear measurable results which makes the reader ready to do business with you? Do you know the cost of

conversion for each advert and your ROI (return on investment)?

2. **Direct Mail:** Do you know your demographics inside out and where to find and reach your target market?

3. **Your Website:** Is it working hard enough for you or is it in need of a major workout? How good are your search engine rankings? Are all your tags installed effectively? Are you tracking and analysing your site visitors and do you know how many are converting to paying customers?

4. **Email Campaigns:** Are you building relationships with your customers and sending them value-adding information on a regular basis in the form of a regular newsletter or blog.

5. **Telephone:** Do you routinely spend time on the phone to your customers to increase your revenue and maximise your earning potential?

6. **Press Releases:** Are you exposing your business to the National and local media in order to position yourself as an expert in the industry?

7. **Alliances:** Who is in your gang and who else would you like to be in your gang?

8. **Referrals:** Are you getting enough of them and if so how are you rewarding the referring customer?

Now be honest with yourself - how many of the above do you systematically use to entice your customers to use your face painting service?

Maybe at this point you're thinking "Yeah, but all this marketing stuff costs a great deal of money". Well let me tell you that that's where you're so very wrong, and I'd like to dispel that illusion. There are many ways that you can market your business successfully without breaking the bank to do so. If you have a low budget then there are low-cost strategies for you to use and some are even free and you'll only need to be testing in order to find the ones that work out for you. What you'll need to be spending though is time, and sometimes plenty of it. The time and persistence spent on your marketing activities will show a great return and more profitable income streams. So are you going to make that informed decision to take action with your marketing? I hope so, as there is probably so much untapped potential in your business which can be yours if you're prepared to work hard for it.

Now on the other hand you might be saying here that business is plentiful, can't book another event, you are already a supreme marketer, and all that jazz. That's great - but did you know that as good as your business is, every aspect of your business still has room for improvement and then it should be improved again. After your improvements have been made you should immediately start looking to improve them once more. Don't stand still and don't ever become complacent. Take a long critical look at all your systems and how you operate, and always have an open mind to new opportunities for taking your business one step further. If you are fully booked and can't possibly take on any new business, then the obvious answer here is it's time to recruit and train more staff to take you to the next level. That's what happened to me in my business over twenty years ago – so I took on extra staff to help with the demand of bookings that were coming in. I trained them up to our standards and they were then able to attend events on behalf of the company. It was not unusual during the high season summer months to have six events running in one day covered. All that only happened because I made a decision to make it happen.

Set Yourself a Marketing Plan

So how do you initially get yourself going with this 'marketing thingy' and propel yourself into the same league like the big guys? The one and only answer is to become a master marketer – it really is as simple as that! So like I've said quite a few times before, because I need to hammer it home, put down your face paints and focus all your creative energy into setting yourself a sound marketing plan.

You need to try out as many marketing activities as you can for your face painting business – but remember, always on a small scale first. Also don't put all of your eggs into one basket at the same time and your energy into one marketing element because if it's no good and it flops then that will be a whole lot of wasted time. You need to be testing a variety of things all at once. If a particular campaign was successful, keep doing it, and each time roll it out on a bigger scale.

Before you set your marketing plan into action you need to ask yourself some simple questions:

- What sets you apart from your competitor that makes you unique from them? Are you different? How are you different?

- Are you clearly communicating all the benefits of your service to your customers, Do they know how you're going to add value to their lives?

- Do you copycat what your competitors do with regards to advertising, promotion and pricing? If it's good enough for them, is it good enough for you. Really? Or are you wasting money just like them?

- Does your current advertising make the reader eager to do business with you? Do you know the cost of conversion from the adverts that you place?

How did you answer? Were you able to answer? Do you feel that you're ready for a change in the way you market to your customer?

A really great marketing exercise to do is to critically analyze your working environment, maybe your face painting stall/booth where your customer spends their time with you. Is everything you see around you geared to help and aid with your selling process? Is it marketing to your customer? Do you have promotional material on view for them to look at as they wait in line? I hope so.

With that in mind, think about the time you've been waiting for an appointment at the Doctor's, the Dentist's, the hairdressers or the pizza shop. What do they have on offer for you to read as you wait? Magazines, plenty of magazines. Why are they filling your mind with irrelevant information that isn't about them and their business and what they can offer to you, their customer? Waiting areas should be filled with positive information about the company - portfolios of photographs, case studies, testimonials and letters from customers and suppliers and even certificates of achievement. When people are in your establishment, your area so to speak, you don't want them to be doing anything else other that looking and reading about what you do, the benefits your service has to offer them and being communicated to in a way that motivates them into making an enquiry, an event booking or a purchase of some sort.

Before we get onto the 'where to advertise' in the next few chapters let's get onto the 'how to advertise'. Your advert, regardless of whether it's in a community magazine, information on your website, or on the back of a bus, must be clear to the reader about what it is you want them to do. So what do you want them to do? You want them to contact you of course. Easy. If they don't telephone you, email you, text you, or write to you as soon as they see your advert – they are very unlikely to do business with you and become your customer. So that's your main point for placing an advert, any advert whether it's offline or online, to get those prospective customers to get in touch with you now_so they can hear all about what it is that you have to offer them.

Attention Grabbing Headlines

So first things first – the headline. This is essential to get right when designing your adverts as this could be the make or break with regards to your potential customer reading on. You want your headline to entice them in so that they continue to read the rest of the advert, right through the copy, right down to the call to action. If you've got your call to action just perfect your customer may not even get that far if you've got a lousy headline. People are in a hurry these days and most just scan adverts in newspapers and magazines, only reading the headline, and if the headline isn't screaming benefits, benefits, benefits then their eyes will wander on to the next advert in view and yours will be long gone I'm afraid.

Good headlines will make your reader curious to know more. You could start with an announcement for something new or undiscovered in mainstream party entertainment. Your headline could ask the reader a question like 'What if ....' and get them to mentally answer it. Another good headline is the 'How to' headline. People like being told how to do certain things in a certain way, especially if it's going to make their life easier. Remember that the main purpose of your headline is to get the readers to read on through the rest of your advert.

So what's an example of a boring headline?
• Face Painting at Your Child's Party

A much better example of the same headline would be:
• The Essential Ingredient For Your Party – Face Painting to Transform the Kids at Your Party into

Tigers, Butterflies, Superheroes and Fairies (the customer sees a picture in their mind).

Make your headlines so interesting that your reader will be compelled to read on. Your titles should be about how to overcome something. It needs to grab attention. It needs to answer the question "What's in it for me".

Below is a list of a dozen headlines that would have massive impact in your advertising:

- The 5 Steps to Selecting a Great Face Painter (and then list them)

- Discover How to .... so that you never have to............... (could be about how to keep children entertained at their party)

- The 12 ways you can benefit from ......[having a face painter in attendance at a company event to hook in customers]

- What is The Best (Worst, Hardest, Lousiest) Way to Organise a Children's Birthday Party? [tell them how]

- What Do You Like (Need, Love, Hate) The Most (Least, Worst, Best) About Holding a Children's Birthday Party at Home? [list the benefits, reasons, fears]

- We're very excited about .....[launch something new/review something that is topical in the news that is relevant to face painting]

- Hot Off The Press. Discover brand spanking new ....[a new service/face painting design]

- If You've Been Searching (Looking) For .... Then We Have The Answer [the benefits of booking a face painter]

- This Seasons Trends in Face Painting are ..... [list them]

- There's More Than One Way to Entertain the Kids at Your Party (Event, Promotion, Fun Day) [tell them what it is]

- How to Organise Your Party (Event, Fete, Fun Day) so that you always .... [lists the benefits]

- Top Seven Reasons to Book a Face Painter For Your Party (Event, Fete, Fun Day) [list the 7 reasons]

Try using power words in your headlines such as:

Compelling, Crucial, Essential, Explosive, Fantastic, Impact, Massive, Revealed, Eliminate, Secret, Smart, Presenting, Introducing, Eliminate, Abolish, Remove, Reduce, Discover, Find Out, Learn, Realise, Uncover, New, Innovative, Fresh, Recent, Latest, Modern.

Have a go at writing fifty different headlines, yes fifty and decide on the single best one. Make them striking, interesting, attention grabbing and thought provoking. Don't throw the others away though as these can be stored in a file to pull out and use as inspiration another day. On one occasion it took four hours for my husband and me to write the headline of a single press release because we wanted to get it just right. In your file also keep cutting examples of other headlines that people have used that you can pull out for motivation.

Copy Writing – not to be confused with Copy Right!

The words you write whether on an advert, on your posters and other sales material or on your website must persuade the reader to get in contact with you. It's all about taking the reader through a journey of powerful evoking word pictures that shows them how their life would be easier, improved, complete, productive, fulfilled or whatever if they did business with you. Your face painting service may help them to save time, save money or save worrying. Write your copy so that it resonates with the reader, write in the way that they would write and keep a conversation tone going rather than a formal editorial piece which may be off-putting to them.

It's true, the copy in your adverts should contain AIDA (get their Attention, make them Interested, give them a Desire to buy from you and then finally give them the Action they need to do to contact you) but it goes a lot further than that. Your copy should sell the end result, sell the benefit and above all sell the emotion. Statistics show that all buying decisions are 80% emotional – how it'll make the consumer feel.

People are so busy these days and are faced with information overload wherever they look. So much information at their fingertips, too much information to take in all at once. We have all become conditioned to scan-read, skipping through big chunks of text for isolated words that are beneficial to us, that resonate with us, that will give us what we're looking for. Your words that you write need to jump out from the page, they need to make the reader stop in their tracks and take time to actually read the full paragraph or advert. So make sure you put the crucial piece of information first that you want to get across to them because if you take a long time getting to the point with too much waffle you'll lose the readers interest in a flash. Keep sentences short as well and use bullet points that are easily read and picked out.

Some good advice and tips on copy writing are:

- Be the prospective customer reading your copy. Does it meet *your* needs, is it what *you* desire, will it fulfil *your* dreams?

- Make the copy simple to read. Don't complicate it with technical jargon or complicated language. Write in conversation tone, as you would speak as if chatting with a friend, using correct grammar and spelling though – not the type you see in text-talk.

- Place the focal point on the benefits and make the features a minimal comparison. When you book the guy to come in and clean your oven, you're not interested in what brilliant cleaning chemicals he uses, you're just interested in how clean your cooker will look so you won't be embarrassed when you have the family round for dinner. Think benefit, benefit, and benefit.

Two hugely powerful words to include in your copy writing is the words You and Your. Make your copy all about them and not just anybody. Open up your webpage now, or a handful of other peoples face painting sites, and you'll find that the majority will be over cramming their site with sentences that start with 'We can do this' or 'We will do that' or 'We have this'. Pages are filled with the word we, we, we. The customer doesn't care about you, that word is not about the customer, it's about the company. Take a long serious look at the copy that you've written and anywhere that it says 'We' change and tweak it to the word You or Your, and make it all about them.

Direct Response Advertising

Okay, so they've read your attention grabbing headline and the content you've written has kept them reading on, next you need to stimulate a response from them, for without a direct response it will be a waste of a good advert and quite unlikely that they will ever become your customer. How many times have you seen an advert for something you'd like, you tear the advert out of the newspaper/magazine, you put the torn piece of paper on the sideboard, in your handbag, on the fridge – and then what? You forget to contact them, you can't be bothered anymore to contact them, and your fleeting desire has passed. The advert stays there for a few weeks gathering dust and then it goes in the bin! Wasted opportunity – the seller didn't make that advert compelling enough for you to contact them immediately so that a sale could be made.

Now the direct response that you want to receive from them can actually be a number of things. Do you want your customer to contact you for a brochure, do you want them to visit your website, do you want them to make a booking for an event, do you want them to receive a free gift or to come along to a service launch party. You could write a special report about something you are most passionate about within the entertainment industry, and use that as a giveaway to anyone that contacts you. There are numerous reasons that you may wish for your customer to get in touch with you – and remember that the more appealing the offer, the more likely it is that they will get in touch (especially if you're offering a free gift, sample or report, etc).

Your direct response can also be for an offer that has a specific deadline, something that needs to be purchased or booked this week or by the end of the month. People move much quicker if you put the scarcity factor into place by letting them know that once it's gone it's gone. Have you purchased something because you've been told there's only so many left, only a few more days remaining to get it at this price or only a limited edition? I bet you have at some time.

After placing your advert and on your customer contacting you it's essential for you to capture their full information, with their permission for future marketing purposes of course. You will need their details so that you can add them to your growing base of potential customers, and then with this information it can be used over time to build a relationship with them by informing them about your products, services, special promotions and packages that we discussed earlier. It's all about building relationships with people and not just trying to sell to them in the first instance. It's worth noting here again that people buy from who they like, know and trust rather than buying cold from an isolated advert. It's wise to put some sort of system in place here for asking people who contact you where they heard about you from. You may have multiple adverts running at one time, or leaflets being picked up at various points, or posters displayed out there in the community, so you'll need to know where the interest is coming from. Devise some sort of document whereby you can capture this information by simply asking "Can I ask where you heard about me from" and log it immediately. Just a simple A4 sheet with your marketing headings written across the top (advert, leaflet, poster, etc) with columns for you to write the customer information in will be all that's needed for you to effectively gauge the responses as they come in.

Keep on track of your sums as well and know how many responses you'll need in order for them to turn into actual customers. Just because you get say ten responses that may not make the cost of the advert worthwhile unless a couple of those responses generates into a booked event or party, and the net profit from those customers are equal to the cost of the advert or is much greater than the cost of the advert. This is where testing (more on this in a moment) plays an important role in your marketing. Test all of your marketing activities on a regular basis – and if it's working then keep on doing it.

Make sure your adverts are influential direct response adverts, as they will produce clear measurable results. Also bear in mind that too much useless information crammed into your adverts or other sales material could inadvertently bombard your customer with visual whiplash. So keep it simple.

The Call to Action

With your direct response advert in place you must let the customer know *how* to contact you, for without it they will be confused and you will end up losing their interest. So a direct response advert means letting the customer know how to contact you right now, yep right now. You might want them to telephone you, to email you, or to go to your website and submit a sign-up form, to name but a few. This is called the 'call to action and is generally found at the bottom of an advert. Whatever is your chosen method, make sure that it is clear and direct about what they need to do, when you want them to do it, and why you want them to do it and of course what's in it for them.

You could put deadlines in your call to action so that people have something to work with. Your offer may be just for the coming weekend or must be used by the end of a particular month, or you could state that you only have xyz left and it goes to the first twenty callers.

By designing your adverts with a direct response in them and a call to action, will automatically give you the evidence as to whether the advert is working or not. No responses will indicate that it was a waste of money because no-one called, compared to a good response of callers meaning that it could potentially be money well spent.

A Load of Old Nonsense

Take a moment here to reflect on how your customers come to you. Was your first thought - "Well I advertise in the local newspaper, or in the local directory, or in the Yellow Pages? That's where my competitors advertise as well and it brings in most of my business". Well let me tell you - don't believe that when you have a business you have to advertise in countless newspapers and magazines in order to be successful. Not only is most paper advertising a waste of time but it will also be very demoralizing for you, as you will feel that your business is worthless if you don't get the response or bookings that you expected. Just because your competitor advertises in a certain publication it certainly doesn't mean that you should as well. Have they been testing and measuring the response of that advert to discover whether or not it is really working for them. Probably not! So don't copy them.

Now let me ask you this. Think about the most recent advert that you placed in any publication. Can you see it in your minds-eye? Where in the publication was it placed? Was it easy to find? Did it jump out from the rest? How many enquiries did you get from that advert and how many bookings were made? What was the customer conversion rate? I'll take a guess here that you don't exactly know! Don't worry though, as most business owners haven't got a clue whether their advertising is working or not! You need also to remember that conversion rates in your marketing can be lower than expected, but when you do secure a new customer they can be worth their weight in gold to you and far outweigh the cost it took to get them in the first place.

To find out for certain how well your adverts are doing, as well as all your other marketing activities, you must TEST and MEASURE all aspects of your advertising campaigns – regularly, without fail.

Testing the Effectiveness of Your Marketing

Never be fooled by placing an advert in a publication and leaving it to run for a couple of months in the hope that it will work. Keep track of it, regularly.

You need to consistently know:

- How many direct responses were made
- How many of those turned into actual customers
- How much income was generated from those customers

- If the profits were greater than the cost of the advert

If any of your advertising isn't working, you must stop the advert immediately. Just by prolonging it by keeping it going isn't going to mean that eventually it will take off because it won't. If it's not working for you now, then it's very unlikely that it won't work at all. Ever! This is a big trap that a lot of face painters fall into. They are under the illusion that to be advertising is a good thing to be doing with no regard as to how efficient that little advert really is. You must, must, must get into the habit of testing and measuring the responses and results of your advertising and make a quick, quick, quick decision as to whether it's viable to carry it onwards and upwards or whether to cut your losses and quit before you waste another whole load of hard-earned money.

Draw out some sort of table matrix that you can use to record all the elements of your advert and stick to tracking the information as it happens. This will provide valuable information for you and will help you to plan any future paper-based advertising campaigns.

The things that you'll need to record on your matrix will be along the lines of:

- The publication *(Village Newsletter)*
- Its verification readership *(1270)*
- The cost of advert *(£98.00)*
- The duration of the advert *(one month)*
- How many other similar advertisers like you *(2)*

- Page number advert placed *(5)*
- Position of advert on page *(top right corner)*
- Colour or black and white *(colour)*

And now for the most important elements to be tested and measured are:
- Your Headline - *what it said*
- Your Copy Writing - *what it read*
- Your Direct Response - *what it was*
- Your Call to Action - *what was used*
- How many enquiries did you receive
- What follow-up process you used
- How many Bookings were made

You should also test different page positions as you'll find that adverts placed on the right hand page tend to be looked at and read more so than those on the left hand page. Even better is to get your advert on the right hand page in the right hand corner. Change the colour and style of your fonts every now and then and use different photos or graphics, or don't use photos or graphics at all. But make sure that you test and record the different ways that you are doing things.

To get a better understanding of your adverts you need to try different publications and different media sources. Try your adverts out on a small-scale basis though, and certainly don't agree to long successive adverts running in one single publication unless you are sure that it is a dead cert and will bring you in a definite return on investment. Speaking of long-term adverts it is imperative that you get your Yellow Pages advert 100% perfect if that's where or you choose to advertise as it's there for a very long time and unchangeable over the duration. I once had a Yellow Pages advert that was the wrong colour shade or red (too much orange) unlike my known branding then, and unfortunately I was stuck with it for twelve months!

By continually testing, recording and measuring each and every advert along with each and every element of the advert will give you a better understanding of what is working and what isn't. Change and tweak your adverts on a regular basis and you'll get a clearer picture of what works and what doesn't. Ditch the ones that are not working hard enough for your money.

- Change things like the headline, and compare to a previous advert.
- Change things like the page placement, and compare.
- Change things like the copy, and compare.
- Change things like the direct response message, and compare.
- Change things like the call to action, and compare.

Don't keep running the same old boring advert that you have been doing for months (or even years) just because it is easy to do so, just because it's less hassle to update, and just because your competitors do! Change it and change it as often as possible (obviously not possible for the yellow pages, however your free listing on yell.com can easily be changed often).

If you test and measure a couple of new marketing strategies each month on a small scale basis, say twenty-four over the year, at the end of that time you should have at least a dozen or so that you know are working, which you can continue with on an ongoing basis and that will be sufficient enough for you to turn your business around. Believe me – it works. You need to be doing many marketing activities all at once and not just paper-based advertising, and testing, measuring and recording the results on each and every one of them. If what you're doing is working and it turns out that you made money, even if it's only a small amount then you need to roll it out on a bigger scale again and again. You must be in a position that you know how much each marketing activity is costing you, how much revenue it's producing and of course how much profit it will make. Likewise stop anything that isn't working.

So to recap – test on a small-scale basis and measure the response. If you made a good return on investment, roll it out again, and again. If it's not – you know what to do!

So with that said, let's get straight on to some great little marketing strategies that I've used on my businesses over the next couple of chapters ....

CHAPTER 12

Advertising Offline

Where To Advertise

We've spent some time looking at how to advertise by using effective direct responses, call to actions and compelling headlines that can be used across the board in all of your sales literature and promotional material. Now it's time to look at *where* to advertise, what different business building principles you can use and how to best market yourself.

Newspapers

You probably have a local newspaper that covers your immediate area and this is a great place to try out paper-based advertising. Give the editor a telephone call to find out if there is a forthcoming feature being run on the party industry, or ask if there is some kind of advertorial that can be run about you, which is a combination of you placing an advert with the publication and them writing some editorial about you.

And don't forget you must remember to make it a direct response advert with a compelling call to action for the prospective customer to make as you will be competing against many, many other advertisers that evening and your advert must stand out from the rest to be in with a chance (remember chip-paper tomorrow)!

There are a number of low-cost publications that you can test the water with, and it's far better to build your advertising up slowly and steadily than to go in at full force and spend your entire marketing budget on just this one strategy alone as there are so many other ones to choose from.

I don't particularly like newspaper advertising because it's expensive and you're in competition with too much other stuff which is a barrier to your advert actually being seen. However it does tend to have a huge reach – but not necessarily to the right target market, yours.

Community Magazines and School Newsletters

Find out if your local neighbourhood has a community magazine – the sort that comes out monthly and covers a widespread area in your location. This type of community magazine tends to stay around on home-owners coffee tables for a while and over the month may be picked up and casually glanced at many, many times, unlike a newspaper that is here today and gone tomorrow.

Contact some of the other trades that advertise in it to get a feel for what you could expect from the publication and find out if they're securing new customers from their advert.

You may again also enquire if the editor of the magazine is interested in doing a piece about you as a feature to go alongside your advert which will go a long way towards your business profile, especially if you're new to the industry.

You could also pop along to as many schools in your area as you can to find out if they're producing a brochure for their school fete. Even if you're unable to face paint there for whatever reason, it's a great publication for you to place an advert into as it's totally geared towards your target market. Unfortunately most schools these days won't allow you to put leaflets and the like into the children's book bags or to even promote yourself on the schools' notice board (unlike the good 'ol days)!

Direct Mail Shots

Traditional direct mail is a bundle of information that you send out to your existing customers or potential customers in the post over a period of time. This can be in the form of a postcard, to a leaflet or brochure to a long sales letter. Either way it's a sales message that you are sending out to a specific group of people. To run a successful direct mail campaign you must send multiple postings to your customer in order for them to sit up and take note. An isolated postcard in the post to them from you outlining any special offers that you're promoting this month has every likelihood of going straight into the waste bin. However if you take time to seriously think about the sequence of your campaign and what you intend to send to your customer over the next two, three and four months you stand a better chance of customer conversion as it has all been carefully planned out. A really good multi-step mailing is to start one in August for Christmas promotions but make sure however that you get your timings absolutely spot on.

The hard truth about direct mail shots is that about 90% of your mailings will go in the bin, but (and here's the best bit) that also means that 10% won't. And out of that 10% (say ten people) a few may only glance at it, a few may read it and a few may respond to it. Now that may seem quite low but it could in fact be a very profitable direct marketing campaign. Its' not down to how many responses you get it's down to whether the quantity of responses were profitable or not. Always test and measure against profit made. That one corporate customer who books your service may far out-weigh the cost of the letter and postage to the whole group you sent out to.

You should always embark on a direct mail campaign on a small scale basis first. Invest only an amount of money that if it didn't work out it would be no big deal to lose, but at the same time large enough to be able to get a couple responses from it. If your small-scale direct mailing has worked then roll it out again and again and increase its size along the way as you continue to do so.

Leaflet Drops

As well as taking your leaflets along with you to all events and parties where you provide your face painting service (I certainly hope you are as standard practice), your leaflets can also be placed at many locations in your community such as nursery schools, children's clothes shops, gymnasiums and public houses to name but a few. It's a nice idea to provide the company that has agreed to display your leaflets with a counter-top Perspex holder for your leaflets to go in as they are less likely to throw your marketing material away if you have gone to this sort of trouble. However, on your next visit to re-stock you may find that it is gathering dust in a corner somewhere – this is the chance you'll have to take!

Posters

Have a go at placing posters in libraries, community centres, recreation clubs and fancy dress shops. You may even find that local shops and stores in your neighbourhood would be happy to promote you, especially if you can make it worth their while with a gift voucher, a value adding plan or referral system (which we'll discuss later).

Postcards

Your local mini supermarket and Post Office will more than likely have a customer notice board where people advertise their unwanted items for sale on postcards. Another great and really cheap place for self promotion. Stick a photo of one of your face painting designs on the card as well.

Stickers

Giving a sticker to each child or adult that you paint is a fantastic and impactful way to promote your company, and what's even better is that they have a very low cost.

The stickers that we use are pretty basic as far as the advertising message goes – they simply say: I've had my Face Painted by Mimicks, Book us for Parties, Events & Fundays, followed by our phone number and web address www.mimicks.co.uk

All painted customers both young and old have a sticker placed on their t-shirt and they leave with our company website information so they can easily source us should they wish to make a booking for their own event in the future. I've had many occasions where parents have booked a year or so after our first point of contact that was made with us as they had stuck our sticker on their fridge. Contact can also be made back to us in the event of any skin irritation or issue arising from the face painting application.

Another great thing about the stickers that we use is that they are individually printed on their own self-adhesive backing. That means that we can collect the sticker backs and count up how many faces were done at each and every event.

My usual system is to record details about every event that we attend and this is how I know that in our peak years of running Mimicks we were painting some 11,000 faces annually. Now that's a lot of painted people over the last two decades!

Stickers are also an invaluable way to help you 'cut off your queue' which was discussed in great detail in my book 'Starting Your Face Painting Business'.

There are many sticker providers to be found on the Internet and my advice to you is to start this promotional system as soon as you can. It works a treat.

Promotional Banners

The big free-standing promotional banners have really come down in price recently and they are a great form of advertising for you at your events. You can put a vast amount of written information on them along with some photographic evidence of your service provision. If you're in a position to be able to buy a couple of banners to use at different types of events it's worth getting one that has the words in large print FREE FACE PAINTING HERE TODAY to use at company paid events.

A printed banner with your logo and contact details will add an extra special and professional touch to your face painting set-up whether it's in a small community village hall or in the reception area at a blue-chip company fun day.

Your Uniform

Most face painters adopt some sort of company t-shirt or sweatshirt and with the huge blank canvas that is on your back that is highly visible to your waiting customers, is a massive marketing opportunity. Don't forget that most of the time you will probably have your back to the audience and what better way than to have your company name, telephone number and website emblazed across your back. You could go one step further by having a call to action printed on that says 'Ask me about face painting at your child's party and receive a 10% discount when you book'. A good statement which has a benefit to the customer.

Your Car or Van

As you travel here and there you will be more highly regarded in your community as the service provider for face painting if you have your company details sign-written onto your car. You probably see it time and time again where you live – builders, florists, gardeners and electricians to name but a few professions will use this form of advertising to get them known around their area. You might not need a gas installer at the moment but the day that your boiler breaks down is the day you say 'Oh yeah, there's that guy I see quite often driving around, I'll call him'.

Make the advertising on your car benefit focused so that you are offering something of value to your potential customer.

Bullet points of what you do are very ineffective unless you have a benefit attached to each one on how it can enhance the life of your customer. Take a look at the sign-written cars and vans as you drive around and reflect on the words that they use, what is the benefit to you, is there one? You'll probably realise here that 99% have no benefits whatsoever.

Raffle Prizes

Most schools holding their summer or Winter Fete, and even the local village committee, are on the lookout for free gifts from local businesses to add to their raffle as a prize. Choose a handful of local events and offer a special Raffle Prize to include say a £20 discount off a Face Painting Party. Make sure you have terms and conditions in place as you wouldn't want the winner to live two hours away! This strategy is also a sure-fire way to get into the school's brochure and advertising.

When I had my Fairytale Children's Party Venue a couple of years ago, we always had a Christmas Grotto and countless schools, nurseries and charities asked for donations of free entry tickets to be entered into their raffles or draws. We found that by giving away one free child's ticket per school the winner of the prize would invariably want to bring along their other children so they would purchase additional tickets to suit their needs. A great and effective way to advertise your business and to generate more income. A win-win situation.

Telephone

Your telephone conversations with your customers should grab their attention and be creative. When making telephone calls remember to introduce yourself and state your reason for calling. Use the customer's name where applicable and listen to their needs and let them talk, regardless of whether you're making the call to the customer or whether they're contacting you. Have some sort of script at the ready that you can follow in order to ask the right questions and gauge the responses from them (however make sure you don't sound like your reading it out in parrot fashion as I'm sure you know how that sounds if someone rattles off a written script). Work out a sequence script for all of your calls and jot down bullet points for your lead conversation. This script can then be typed out and kept in readiness to go through as contact is made.

You could also try this one out. Randomly contact five customers by telephone that you have recently worked for as a courtesy and ask how they enjoyed your service that you provided for them. Find out if you could make any improvements to make the experience better and if they felt that anything was missing from the service. Ask for as much feedback as possible. Don't attempt to sell them anything, nothing at all. By giving excellent customer care you will immediately add value to them and to your business. If you're able to get one out of the five to re-book you without even trying – then that indeed was a great exercise. How much more revenue would that mean to your business if you routinely telephoned all your customers after all their events?

I always make a point of texting my B2B customers on the morning of their event to let them know my expected arrival time. It's then that I offer an additional hour's service (or two hours) at a reduced rate to be bolted onto the end of the contracted time. By sending them a text message you're not putting them on the spot and they have time to mull your proposal over before they reply. They're probably really busy with the preparation of the event and rushing here, there and everywhere. They may worry about the huge crowds attending and will the face painter be able to cope. So yes, they text back and agree to increase your contract time just to be on the safe side. Another win-win situation.

Always remember to test your phone campaigns. Test the time of day that you make the call and also test the day of the week. You could always record yourself to check whether you were clear enough, did you sound too pushy, did you sound generally interested in your customers needs.

Press Releases

With a press release you can end up getting free advertising from National and local television, radio, newspapers, consumer magazines and trade publications. In fact the sky's the limit. The more media that you can expose your information to the better chance you have of actually getting something written about you. Try not to send out isolated press releases because if you've spent a long time working on your headline and content you need to make sure that you roll it out on a big scale to as many media companies as possible.

It's very easy to do and costs virtually nothing, apart from your time to write the release and the cost of the postage and it will bring in extra customers as you brand yourself as an authority.

Publicity in the media is far more powerful than any advertising that you can buy. In the eyes of the reader it gives you more credibility as you haven't paid to be there, and therefore will gain you instant trust. If you can get repeat exposure you'll gain expert status as people will say, wow that woman is in the papers every week, she must be good! People decide who the experts are, and by telling your story and by putting yourself forward has little to do with your actual ability in the face painting industry. Whoever has the attention of the media wins.

Most of the press releases that journalists receive however end up going straight in the bin. Make sure yours isn't one of them. You need to think about the publication that you're targeting and what it offers to their readers, and then think about the journalist and what type of information they need to fill the huge amount of white space they have on their pages that will add value to their reader's lives.

It's worth noting here that journalists are not interested in you or your company history, they don't really want to know how long you've been established or about how amazing you are. They want a meaty story that will be interesting to their readers. So remember that if the headline of your press release goes something along these lines – Face Painting Company celebrates being in business for ten years – that is sure to find its way to the bin, but if the headline were to say – Face Painting Business comes of age and to celebrate the staff are doing a bungee jump with their faces painted red, white and blue is by far a more creative headline and the journalist will surely read on.

The layout of your press release is very important. Start with a small date on the first line and then a large heading that has impact and compels the journalist to read on. Follow this with your press release and then finally a very brief description about you, your company and address. Finish with your contact information and website details. Try to keep your press release to just one A4 page. If you have to use two pages it will tell the journalist that you don't know how to get to the point quick enough and it'll put them off.

Remember that:

- Journalists need plenty of information for their readers, so make sure your press release is meeting those needs.
- Your press releases ideally should be controversial and solve a problem.
- Your press release should be a great source of information on the face painting industry. Position yourself as an expert.
- Your press release can capitalise on recent news topics in the media so act immediately – even if it means writing it just before bedtime.

Think about how impressed your customers would be if they saw your competitor on television, and think about how would that make you feel!

I have a great little story to tell you about the power of press releases, and believe me, if you have not yet given it some thought on how you can get your business into the media, start now as the opportunity is out there for you.

A couple of years ago when the credit crunch had just started and things were full of doom and gloom in the media (not much difference from now) and the news was full of reports on business closures and the dreadful economic downturn, our local TV station did a report on the town where my shop and party venue was located. This report was extremely negative with the emphasis on the demise of the area and the untold quantity of empty shops. Our town was no different from most other towns in the country as the recession was hitting everywhere. I became angered about this TV report. How dare they criticize my town, how dare they say that all businesses there were in trouble and how dare they label the area as a ghost town. I immediately put pen to paper and sat down and wrote a press release stating that the information that had been broadcasted on television had not been the true facts. My retail shop and party venue (in the ghost town) was seeing fast growth in income and customer retention and in fact was making more money now than it ever had!

I sent a copy of this press release letter to the local newspapers, and waited for a response. I didn't have to wait long as the very next day the video crew arrived and filmed me at my Fairy School which I ran in my venue, followed by a further two newspaper interviews. When asked why my business was thriving whilst others around me were collapsing, I told them that it was due to my positive thinking and keeping in contact with existing customers. Within a week I was on the front page of one newspaper and page five of another with my video showing on the news websites. I also received a personal letter from the chief executive of the borough council, thanking me for such kind words about the town!!

It was so refreshing in the weeks that followed as so many people came in to the shop to congratulate me on doing so well in these 'awful times'!!!

I watched the local news and acted on an immediate opportunity to get myself into the newspapers and this is what you must also do. Start looking for opportunities around you, and this will become a massive power of branding as you become a public figure with specialist status. Listen intently at the stories on your local news programmes and ask yourself if there's a problem that you can solve. Maybe you have strong opinion on something topical or can look at an issue through the eyes of an expert. Read newspapers and national magazines, and listen to the gossip in the street and what your customers are saying. All these places could provide you with an ideal opportunity for your press release. All it takes is ONE of those opportunities to get you going. And when you see the impact that it can cause then you'll start doing it more and more. Look for opportunities wherever you can and turn negative situations into positive ones. Everyone loves a 'feel-good' story.

Presentations

Offer to do a presentation talk about your company at local networking groups, mother and toddler groups, brownies and cubs, dance clubs and youth theatres. In fact anywhere that your target market hangs out – ask for a short time-slot of about ten-minutes to give a presentation, to hand out leaflets or to demonstrate your skill.

Awards

Another fantastic way to raise awareness of your business is to enter as many awards as you can. These can be on a local or national basis, to even an international basis. Keep a look out and even search the Internet to find the types of competitions you'd like to enter. Awards can also be nominated to you by your customer recommendations. Not only will this massively boost your self-esteem but will also have a big impact in how you can sell yourself.

Alliances

Forming an alliance, or joint venture, with a complimentary company, say a children's' clothes shop, a fancy dress shop or a balloon modeller is a great way for you both to capitalise on each other's customer lists. A sort of piggy-back relationship. Team up with an allied entertainer; say a clown, so that you can fully promote each other's services to each other's customer list. This could be done through dedicated pages on each other's websites, or leaflets and promo banners. It may also be possible for you to piggy-back onto another entertainer's newsletter campaigns. Try giving away free gifts and coupons for each other's company, try doing a joint promotion (an overall 15% discount if the customer books you and the clown) or you could even spend an afternoon in a fancy dress shop to promote your face painting service, especially around Halloween, and give a percentage back to the shop for every customer who books your service. The list can be quite endless when you put your mind to it.

If you have ten joint ventures or alliances and each one is only minimally productive with say only one new customer coming in each month from each alliance that means that by the end of the year you will have had 120 new customers. Yes 120 new customers. That additional income will be a welcome surprise! Work on some alliances and joint ventures today. Who would you like to have in your gang? Who can help you, and who can you help? Compile a list and include the benefit and impact that they could have over your business.

Reciprocal Referrals and Recommendations

We all know that word of mouth is great for any business, but you need to go one step further in order for you to profit from it by implementing some sort of referral system. I love systems – you've probably realised that by now though! It's all very well that Mrs Jones, your private customer, has been singing your praises to Mrs Smith, but if Mrs Smith does no more than listen to her friend, and not act upon it and make a booking with you, then quite honestly it's a total waste of a good conversation, and breath.

Don't wait for referrals to self-generate, you need to take the bull by the horns and make them happen by giving your customers a good and solid reason to do so. By planting the seed early on in your customer relationship and by providing first-class service results your customer will be only too pleased to pass your information onto their acquaintances who they feel could benefit from the same service that you have provided for them.

Refer and Reward systems are very easy to set up at any stage of your business life, and it goes without saying that the earlier the better. During your event with Mrs Jones you need to slip it into the conversation that you have a referral system in place whereby any customer that refers will be rewarded. Ask Mrs Jones about her friends and family and whether she feels that any one of them could benefit from the same or similar service that you have provided. If she only gives you one name as a referral then that's a start in the right direction. Before you leave the event ask her to write the details of this contact down on your specially prepared referral card. Let her know that if her word-of-mouth generates a new customer for you she'll be legible for a reward from you. This will encourage her even more so to tell her friends all about you and to help spread the good word. Give her a handful of your business cards and leaflets to help with this process.

Now it's most important here to make sure that all new customers who come to you are asked 'How did you hear about me'. That new customer might say from a leaflet that she picked up in the library, by looking at your website, from a networking event or from Mrs Jones down the road. Straight away, there are two opportunities to be rewarded – the library and Mrs Jones.

You'll need to decide what shape and form the reward will be in and how much will it cost for you to implement it. Anything that is non-business or industry related will be seen as a true gesture of good-will as you have gone out of your way to find and purchase the free gift for them. This could include things like a box of chocolates, a bunch of flowers, a cinema ticket, a school uniform voucher, a book voucher (not for the library though) or a restaurant discount voucher. Depending on the nature of the service supplied to your newly referred customer will determine the expenditure you make on the gift to reward the customer who referred. Pack the gift and post straight away to the customer who rewarded and don't forget to include a hand-written note (more personal) of your gratitude. This will do wonders for your business as your customer will feel truly valued and will continue to recommend you to others, and each time she does, you reward with a different gift.

If Mrs Jones is good enough to refer a new customer each and every week then the gift rewards must keep coming each and every week. Never miss or never forget. She'll be so impressed by your system and the fact that a little freebie arrives frequently that she'll continue to sing your praises on a regular basis and as loud as she possibly can. Again this is another win-win situation you can find yourself in!

As your business grows along with your customer list you will find that by providing a good face painting service will bring about recommendations to others from those who have been happy with the quality that you provide. Word of mouth is by far the best form of advertising that you could ever wish for. The words spoken by others about you hold more influence and will have much more impact than anything you could ever write in an advert or say about yourself.

CHAPTER 13

Advertising Online

Your Online Presence

Online marketing is by far one of the most profitable marketing strategies that there is for your face painting business and it's without a doubt my most favourite form of marketing. This is a huge area to explore and when done properly it can be extremely profitable for you. Your online marketing should be put on consistent auto-pilot where possible and become systematic in defining what problems your customers are having so that you can solve them and put a marketing plan in place.

Website Creation

To be in business without a website is like being a window cleaner without a ladder. The two go together, hand-in-hand. Always have, always will. You should, however, have your *own* website, and not one of these free ones that have adverts and pop-ups, and not just space either on any of the chat forums like Facebook, MySpace and Bebo. You need your *very own creation*, your own shop window for your customers to look into.

In this day and age you will find that before a customer does business with you, they will want to check you out first before contacting you by telephone or email to see what you're all about. Even if you come highly recommended – they will still like to get a visual feel for you before they strike. Gone are the days when a brochure or leaflet would suffice. People are hungry for a lot more information and they have a lot more choices out there – so make sure you're up there with the rest of your competition, or you won't get a look in. Your very own shop window will become a place for people to browse into at their leisure so your website should be properly dressed with the correct information and pricing so that it is a desirable place to be for your customer in this Internet shopping mall.

Website marketing, when done properly can be extremely profitable as it's not that difficult to rank high in the search engines for your local area, or to track and analyse your site visitors in order to see just how many are converting to customers if you know how to do it effectively.

If you choose a web designer to create your website you need to make sure that there is a content management system in place, and you would need to know if there are any restrictions on the frequency of updating your site and of course how much this will cost you. Don't believe though that you have to have a professionally built website by a web designer in order to compete on the Internet. Another route to follow would be to design the website your-self using a software programme such as Dreamweaver or WordPress. This will give you greater control of how you manage your site with regards to updating the content (which incidentally should be done regularly in order to stay on top of the search engine rankings). You will also have more control over installation of your autoresponder, PayPal buttons and site statistic analyzers.

If producing your own website you'll spend a considerable amount of time in building and designing it and one of the most overlooked facts is how you're going to let people know that you're out there. When you move home do you send people that you know a postcard to inform them of your new address or do you just let them play the guessing game and hope that with trial and error of going down every close, avenue and road in the neighbourhood where they think you might be living they will eventually stumble across your new home by accident!! This is so very true for your website. You do the rough draft, you then design it, you then get it hosted, and you then wait for the business to come flooding in. But no one comes. No one knows you're out there.

A major way to get your site noticed is through your search engine optimization, SEO, which is something that you should commit to yourself as once you get the hang of it; it becomes second nature as you build your website. Don't be fooled by sales reps when they telephone you saying that they can guarantee you high rankings and page one on Google. This is totally untrue as no one can guarantee you space at the top. You must let the world and its brother know where you are through your title pages, your alt tags, your keywords and keyword-phrases, your hyperlinks, your inbound and outbound links and of course your offline advertising. Wow that's a long list isn't it – and the bottom line is, it has to be done if you want to be found. Avoid having a hush-hush website that no-one can find. I run small group workshops in the above methods and if you feel that your website needs a workout please email me for details at info@mimicks.co.uk

Before you go ahead and design your website you must know what its purpose is. Is it just a shop window, will you be selling from it, is it an information site, is it there to build relationships with potential customers. You'll probably find that your website will have one key element overall which is to convert visitors into buying customers. Most visitors arriving at your website have done so because they chose to – so don't let them leave. Reinforce their time with you by giving them enticing and interesting items to read. You can accelerate your expert status with articles, reports, statistics, free gifts, competitions and any other information relevant to the face painting industry. Your site must be full of exciting information that your visitor will find constructive. You have eight seconds to make a first impression with a visitor to your website before they click through to another site and bounce right out. Not long, eh!! So make sure you are giving them what they have come for, immediately, or else they will just move on and they'll probably be gone forever.

If your visitors are arriving on your site via a landing page, from either search results, directory listings, social media links or domain strings then make sure that these pages give clear and simple instructions as to what the visitor needs to do.

Remember direct response advertising – what do you want your visitor to do. Your landing pages don't need to be over flashy with mountains of copy. Keep them clean and keep them simple. Give the visitor limited choices in what they should do next or too many options will add to confusion and they'll leave your site in a clickety-click. If a landing page is also a sign up page for them to add their details for your newsletter only give them two options – either sign up or to go. This is known as a squeeze page. Give your customer an incentive to take action now, make it clear and make it compelling for them to do so.

If people purchase your face painting service directly from your site, by either paying a booking deposit or by paying in full you're always going to get anxiety issues with a number of your customers. These anxieties will include can they trust you, what about credit card security, is it value for money, what is your reputation like. You need to reduce and eliminate these fears by offering a guarantee (more on that later) by also adding testimonials as they are social proof and full contact information on every single page of your site. By having your contact details on every single page, if the customer wishes to telephone you or to email you and they would like to do that now, they haven't got to go searching for your contact information. You could also put your telephone number under certain paragraphs throughout your site in a small font and in a lighter colour to the body text. Try it and see what happens. Test, test and then test again! Privacy policies are also good however they can be over negative and this could put your prospective customer off. It's always a good idea to have an

About Us page which outlines a brief summary of who you are and this will make you become a real person.

When starting to build your site don't fall into the trap of running out of time or motivation to see your project through. Persevere. Blank pages on your website that are 'under construction' will send out a message that you're not on top of your game and will be just like having a naked mannequin in your shop window that people do a double-take to. Make sure all your content is complete before uploading it and think twice about putting a 'naked' page out there.

By designing your own site will benefit your cash flow in the long run as you will not need to keep paying your designer to update your site for you, and you will also be able to test and measure its performance easily, quickly and whenever you feel the need. So what are the fundamental elements that you should be testing on your site, and what results should you be recording?

1. Well number one is clearly your traffic. Test how many visitors are being attracted to your site and where they came from, and how did they find you. Did they come via a search engine or was it their keywords and key-phrases that they used? How many bounces do you get? A bounce incidentally is when visitors come into your site and very quickly go back out again.

2. Test the activity of the pages they are visiting once they are there, and how do they navigate your site?

3. Test your conversion rates on how many visitors you had to how many became actual paying customers.

4. Test different headlines and test different copy. If you do this regularly you will be able to pinpoint what works and what doesn't.

5. Test the offers and gifts that you are giving to your customers.

6. Test Pay Per Click advertising and Adwords.

7. Test article marketing by submitting to article directories.

Your website should be improved and updated on a regular basis – at least once a month, but weekly is more ideal. Test changing the front page from its usual layout. Change the headlines and tweak the body text. Change the colours, sizes and styles of your fonts. This process is ongoing and should never end or be put on the back burner.

You could have the best face painting website in the world with finely crafted headlines, excellent content, fantastic photographic evidence and compelling call to actions which entice in a flood of visitors – but if you aren't keeping track of results and daily activities, then quite honestly you're not helping with your online presence.

I make it a regular discipline to track, measure and record all the following areas of my websites:

- How long the visitors stay on my site
- What pages they visit when they are there
- How they found me, search engine, direct link, etc.
- What location or country they are they from
- How they navigate my site
- What keyword searches they use

... and that's just for starters!

So perhaps now is the best time to install a website analyser in order to track the effectiveness of your site and its pages to give you a better understanding of what your potential customers are looking for, and what they are doing. You may find that you have a high bounce rate on one of your pages meaning that this page isn't working to its fullest potential, as it's not holding your visitors interest. You'll get a better understanding of all the pages on your site and will be able to plan for any improvements. Once you get going with your analyser you will gradually begin to understand the behaviour patterns of your visitors and what makes them convert into a customer. By tweaking, changing and updating your sites content on a regular basis will not only help with your search engine rankings, but will also make for a better visiting experience for your visitor. Your website will become more influential in a way that you control and it will work hard for its keep and not just become yet another stagnant site out there in cyber-space!

Take a long hard look at your website (if you have one already) and do a checklist of all those key areas that you should be testing and recording results on, on a regular basis and after you've done that make sure that your site is as optimized as you can possibly make it and then submit it – with confidence - to the search engines. You've spent good money on your website or many hours of manual labour getting it ready and getting it out there, so don't leave it to chance and hope that your window shoppers are okay when they're spending time with you. Check it out and check it often!

Online Directories

Don't forget to take advantage of the many trade related directories that hold a presence on the internet. Simply search for these by placing a keyword followed by directory i.e. "entertainer's directory" (remember to use "quotes" to prevent having to trawl through a load of random searches) and add your face painting company information to as many as possible of these. It will take a little time to do but believe me it's time well spent.

Some will allow you to add photographs and editorial copy, and some are even happy for you to provide a link back to your website. The majority of directories are free for you to add your details to and some may ask for a small annual fee for inclusion, either way they're a really good platform for you to use to get your message across to your potential customer. Another great feature of directories is that it is a form of viral advertising as other directories will seek you out and add you unknowingly to their very own directory, and so the process goes on and on and you can end up being listed on many, many directories without having to do the legwork!

Social Networking

Social networking is a fabulous way to promote yourself and your business. By using Facebook, Twitter, Linkedin and Pinterest will give you a huge opportunity to sell yourself to your customers. It's on here that you can promote special offers, new products and service information and to place yourself as an expert in your field by sharing top tips and tricks of the trade.

If you decide to get a specific Facebook Page or Twitter account using your business name then go for it – blow your trumpet as loud as you can to engage your captive audience and on a daily basis post events, happenings, discounts, promotions, launches, elite packages, photos and as many top tips as you possibly can. If you have a blog that can automatically be fed through to your social media accounts then do that too.

Remember to put your fair share of usual posts that aren't just business related otherwise you'll be perceived as dull and only business focused. By doing this, sharing a few snippets of your personal life about your family and pets if you have them will make you become a 'real' person that your customers can relate to. Get the mix right and this can be a great arena to help grow your business. You'll need to keep your personal profile and business page separate though as you may not wish for your customers to be informed about any boozy nights out!!!

To find out more about successful social media marketing visit **www.Face PaintingForProfit.co.uk** (not.com)!

Email Marketing

Your existing customers can provide you with rapid growth to your business almost immediately. They have bought from you once before so they trust you as a service provider. You can continue to build a relationship with them over the coming weeks, months and years on the basis of your research into what they want, what are their unfilled needs and what strong desires they have at that moment. Email marketing has proven to be a real cutting-edge approach and you'll not believe the intensity of it until you've tested it and measured its response rate.

Email marketing shouldn't be used to just primarily sell your service as it should be used as a relationship-building tool. How often have you received an email from your hairdresser who is just bursting at the seams to give you advice on the newest shampoo and hair care treatment that's just hit the high street or from your Dentist reminding you that it's smile week and how to promote a healthy brush routine? Probably never, but how effective would that be and how would that make you feel? The hairdresser and the dentist aren't selling anything, nothing at all – they're just keeping in touch, building a relationship with useful snippets of information that is of relevance and of interest to you.

You can very easily adapt an effective email marketing campaign and decide on how often you are going to send out valuable information to those customers who have purchased from you before, which will in turn lead to further purchases of your services or products.

Your email campaign could be a monthly newsletter, or a special report on the entertainment/event industry that you can mail to your customers. If you have difficulty thinking of fresh content, start asking your customers what they would like to know about. Research that information for them and then inform them of it. Devise a product or service based on their answers and market to them straight away. Include tips and advice, take excerpts from your trade magazines and use them as articles (noting the author source). Contact an alliance of the industry and ask if they would like to place a small article within your newsletter. Hold competitions – colouring competitions are good for children to participate in. The list can be endless when you put your mind to it.

Let them get to know you so that they understand that the information you have to offer them is of value and you're not just going for the hard sell. Send them advice, recommend a product and even send them to a link where they can receive a free gift voucher and this will go a long way to them having trust in what you do.

Great ideas for your newsletter could include:

- A write-up from an expert in the face painting industry
- Articles taken from newspapers about children's entertainment
- A report on entertainment crazes from local websites
- Party or event statistics you may read about in a newspaper
- Read a good book and write a review on it
- Watch a film at the cinema and write a review

- Publish the school holiday dates, the library opening times, what's on at the cinema. Endless!
- Send them a cup-cake recipe
- Try out a new product that isn't related to your industry and write all about it, like a face cream or a sun-tan lotion
- Recommend another entertainer and report on how brilliant they are
- Provide a recommended list of websites that you have visited that have great information that you'd like to share, not necessarily industry related
- Discuss your latest face painting design especially if it's a hot topic with children at that moment in time
- Discuss a product range that you're using and give a complete outline of its benefits to the customer
- Write a story about the funny things kids say – like 'Mum can I get my Pace Fainted'!
- Send them a party planning list
- Send them ideas for party games and activities
- Send them ideas for party food and celebration cakes
- Send them a list of the local community centres and halls contact and pricing information

OMG there's so much information at your fingertips that you can use to benefit and enrich your customer's lives with. The information that you send them will be welcomed and they'll look forward to seeing your name in their inbox.

Many restaurant owners use their email campaigns in a most successful manner to send free meal gift vouchers to customers just before their birthday. The offer is for a free meal for the birthday person and as no one generally dines alone on their birthday, there is a good chance that they will bring extra full paying friends with them. This is a win-win situation, the owner wins and the customer wins, and it also provides the restaurant owner with the opportunity to obtain some more email addresses along with birthday dates to put into the system and start the whole process again. WOW, what a fantastic system!! And for you as a service provider there are vast opportunities here for you to think about and unfold as well.

When emailing to your customer database make sure that you put the full URL link to your website at the signature section in your newsletter as you'll want to entice your customer back onto your website. You could even try not writing the complete article or story in your newsletter and have a clickable link back to your website that says click here to read the rest of the story. In your signature section (sometimes called resource box or bio box) you could also write "Do you have a question – click here to email, which takes them straight through to a contact page on your website.

Now in order to have a great email campaign going you need to have a database of customers, but don't worry if you haven't started one yet as from now on in you must make it a requirement to capture as many email addresses as you can from your enquirers, your bookers, your existing customers and through the visitors on your website. If you don't do this the opportunity could disappear for you to start building a relationship with these people and you're throwing away a golden opportunity to sell to them at some stage in the future.

You must, must, must however have permission to add customer email addresses to your database so you either need to ask for permission by explaining what your intentions are or the better method is to get them to fill in their information on a sign-up form that is situated in your website. This sign-up form is usually hosted by a third-party (a communication provider that supplies you with an autoresponder) and the customer will need to confirm her details by opting-in to your newsletter. Another great thing about autoresponders is that your messages to your customers can be personalised with their name so when you hit the send button for your newsletter to be emailed out to your complete customer database, each one will land in their inbox with their own personal name on it. You'll be able to try out using different combinations such as Dear Sally, Hello Sally, Hi Sally or just Sally to see which ones work best for you.

Do be aware that the more information fields that you include in your sign-up form up may become a barrier to the visitor as they may not be happy to give too much information, so simply asking for their name and email address is usually more than enough. However if it is a simple and easy process you will unfortunately attract many people that are not necessarily your target market which you may not want. If you'd like to qualify your customers you can ask a series of additional questions other than just their name and email address and the sign up process takes longer to complete. This way you'll get a far better qualified customer as they are more genuine. Always make sure that you offer something of value to your sign ups like a free report or discount voucher. Ideally sign-up boxes should be positioned at the top of your web pages to grab attention and never hidden away at the footer. Take a random look at six different websites that are not necessarily in our face painting industry, and note what they ask for when completing their sign-up box and where their sign-up boxes are positioned on their websites.

Once you have your email campaign up and running you need to test it on a weekly, fortnightly or monthly scale, to see what works best for you and your customer. Try to keep the style of you email consistent but don't be afraid of changing the content from a long one to a short one and from an information article to a sales article. You need to get the balance right here as you don't want to be bombarding your customer with sales material all the time and only occasionally value-adding articles. Your customer will too easily ask to be unsubscribed from your list if this is the case. So remember – more information based articles and a lot less of the sales pitch.

Remember to regularly test and track your email campaigns and if you have a good autoresponder there should be a report/analytics area where you can track:

- What time did the email arrive in their inbox
- How many emails were actually opened
- Did they forward it on to another person
- How many bounces did you have
- How many enquiries it generated

You should also track yourself as to:

- How many sales were made
- How many leads and referrals came in

Devise a one-year plan on how you're going to communicate with your customers. Plan out a rough draft of the email sequences that you're going to send and include topical articles and information that relates to specific times in the calendar such as Easter, school holidays, Halloween, Christmas, etc, etc. Ideally you need to plan your email marketing sequences well in advance and decide on how often you are going to send out to your database. Another great thing about autoresponders is that you can add all your newsletters into it at once and schedule in specific times for them to be sent out to your list.

Your email campaign is a communication device and a means of building relationships with your customers with you being the master of information that will add value to their lives. Keep your customers well informed with articles of interest and they will look forward to receiving them and not click away at the sight of your name in their inbox. Many of my customers say how much they look forward to my emails as it keeps them fully informed and up to date. Your emails need to be imaginative, diverse, captivating, appealing and humorous – totally unlike any others that they receive. This has been an extremely rewarding part of both of my entertainment businesses – my fairytale party venue and my face painting company and by putting into place an effective email marketing campaign I was able to increase my yearly turnover by 28%. All down to email marketing.

You too can gain immense profit by implementing some simple email marketing tactics into your business bringing in extra revenue that your customers would otherwise be spending elsewhere. Relationships with your customers can be your biggest asset if nurtured correctly.

The information I've supplied you here on online marketing is quite frankly a drop in the ocean as there is so much more out there for you to use in your face painting business like I've done that will help you to attract high value returning and paying customers to your website. But that of course is another book from me!

CHAPTER 14

Sales Process

Would You Buy Your Face Painting Service?

If you were the customer, would buying your product or service be the right choice to make or is there a better option available in the market place. Think long and hard about why your customer should do business with you and not your competitor, what are you offering that they aren't? You must be able to answers these questions positively because if you can't it will mean that you haven't sold the idea or concept to you yet and that's a big problem to face. An important sale to make is selling you on you. Do you believe in yourself and what your business stands for? Do you have self-esteem in what you do? Are you confident and enthusiastic? How do you perceive your own self-image? If you shy away when enquiries are made from customers then you need to re-visit your purpose for being in business, and go and purchase my other book 'Starting Your Face Painting Business'. If you don't have confidence in what you do how on earth can you expect your customers to?

You should also be able to make sure your customers are qualified to sell to as you can't sell vintage champagne from a market stall. You must decide that it's ok to sell to them and definitely don't waste time trying to sell to those who don't qualify because they're looking to bag a bargain. Are they suitable and are they going to purchase at the right price.

Are you following up on each enquiry that you get in your face painting business with a solid sales system, or are you one of those business owners who receive a call from an interested customer, deals with the enquiry and never do anymore than that? This is where you can excel with an outstanding sales process behind you.

When a customer has responded to an advert of yours, whether it's a paper-based advert or from a poster placed in the local community hall or from a leaflet given out at a child's party – have you got in place an efficient sales process? Think about it now – what does *your* sales process entail?

An exceptional sales process could go along these lines:

- Advert placed in a publication or leaflet handed out.
- A new customer telephones to enquire about what you can offer them.
- You discuss their requirements in detail and offer advice. They may book you in this first point of contact, if not:
- You ask for their email address or direct them to your website where they'll see your sign-up form. They may then book you, if not:

- You send them some information, reports, incentives - all value adding. They may then book you, if not:
- You continue to build a relationship with newsletters

- Over time, and after they've gotten to know you they could book your service. You've built the know, like, trust factor.

This is just a generalized process. In order to surpass what you already do you would need to list each and every step of your process and improve on each and every element. You need to think to yourself – how can I make this better for the customer, how can I add more value for them, how can I improve on my customer care. Small improvements that you make can be the page of the website that your direct them to, the words that you use when you first speak with them to the free special report that you send out to them. If you make small incremental changes to each element in the way that you do business with your customer, you'll possibly see changes in peoples buying decisions as they happen.

All of your contact steps should be recorded and monitored to enable you to see your actual conversion rate and at what stage of the process it's likely to take place. By doing this you will have a better understanding of your sales process and what it will take to convert to a sale.

Its wise noting here again like I've done in a previous chapter that peoples' buying decisions differ vastly and it could take a number of contacts between you and the prospective customer to secure the booking for a party or event. Your customer will indeed go on a journey to buy from you rather than making an instant decision. The words "No not now" or "No not today" can eventually make you money. No is not forever, as No just means not this moment in time. We all say no and then change our mind due to our circumstances. Become positive about no not today as it means that the customer will just be put back into your sales process and you can start it all over again with them. People these days lead extremely hectic lives and most of the time they have an awful lot going on. Booking your service today may not be their number one priority as they have a great deal to get done, but in time priorities and state of affairs change and they may well come back to you, as long as you have given them something of value to remember you by. You need continuous ongoing contact as the customer might not buy today, tomorrow or even next month, but with continuous contact they could buy next year.

Think of how you make decisions on buying something. When you buy a new piece of furniture do you buy the first dining table that you see? Of course you don't, so you enter into a buying process, which will be something like this:

1. Decide you need a new dining suite
2. Look in some magazines and/or surf the web
3. Think about the price you can afford
4. Go to a showroom, speak to a sales person and take away a brochure
5. Look at the brochure and price compare on the Internet
6. Go back to the showroom
7. Make a decision

8. Buy the furniture or start the whole process again

If the above scenario was for a customer seeking a face painter for their event then you would come into their lives at point 4. They decide they need party entertainment, they surf the Web, they think about their budget, they contact you. Don't forget that they've already gone through steps 1-3 and at number 4 you will be right there with your competitors, so it's at this point you must be ready to make a good impression. This is where you become a mountain of knowledge and answer all their questions, meet their needs, explain the benefits of what they have chosen and guide them gently through the whole buying decision development. And then this is where you need to capture the details of your customer in order to put them into your sales process.

Most one-stop selling doesn't work, i.e. one point of contact, one phone call, one visit to your website. You need to have a multi step marketing system with your customers as their buying patterns are like a rotating cog-wheel – each click will move them closer to the sale. Whether its six steps or twenty-six steps, follow up with a set process to your enquiries. You have an absolutely perfect reason to keep in contact with people who make enquiries with you. When Mrs. Jones telephones to enquire about little Johnnie's pending party, ask if she would like to be added to your list so that she can receive information and special offers from you by the way of a regular newsletter.

Make a list of your usual multi-step sales process (it may however be only two steps at the moment) and decide on small changes to improve on each element. Next add some new steps to your process to really push for the maximum exposure and then as before continue to change and improve. Also include the following information:

- The scripts you will say on the phone and your leading questions.
- The information you will send out to them for free, to add value.
- The information you will gather on them to use at a later date.
- The timings and procedures of your follow-ups.

Devise some sort of table that you can use as a checklist and diary for incoming enquiries and to record your actions. Any customer that make a provisional booking with you (because they need to chat it over with hubby first) put onto a list and then follow-up with them a couple of days later. We do this and can usually convert 90%. Review your sales process on a regular basis so that it never becomes stale.

Important steps to take when selling to customers and how to influence them is to allow the customer to ask questions, as many as possible. You can also prompt for information by asking open-ended questions such as "what other entertainment or party games will you be organising to run alongside the face painting activity?" that will encourage them to speak and you'll be able to get a good understanding of what it is they're wanting. Don't start telling people about what you do and how great you are and how fantastic your service is until you have answered all their questions and have found out what's important to them. Then hand-pick from your services what you perceive is of being the greatest value to that customer. Incidentally, please don't take this to the extreme whereby you don't blow your own trumpet about how good you are – it's all about keeping the balance right with regards to letting them talk to find out what they want and then letting them know that you're able to fill all those needs by telling them what you can do for them.

When dealing with person to person (and not over the phone) use good body language. Breathe at the same rate as them and speak with the same volume and tone and this will certainly bring a sense of rapport between you (it works and it's quite a fun thing to do)! Look relaxed and open to questions. Nod your head in the right places and be genuinely interested in what your customer is saying. Your customer will immediately pick up on it if you look even slightly disinterested or are unsure on how to answer certain questions. If you have people working for you make sure they are aware of this too. Try testing a few body language postures on a friend or family member and you'll find that it is really easy to do and it's so very effective. Google up body language to get some ideas of what you can do to promote effective communication.

You will of course come across objections - objections to price, objections to perceived value and objections to your product or service - and when you hear them you need to be ready with your answers. Make sure that you continually ask questions and really, really listen to what the customer is saying. Don't beat-about-the-bush. Tell them how it is. This is always a good time to pull out some testimonials from satisfied customers, which will reinforce what you're offering them. If they say that they can't afford it, you then know that their objection is to price so you can then re-establish the value that it will make to them. Keep a running list of the objections that you get and write down the answers to these objections as a sort of script which will become a great resource for you. You may be lucky and they purchase from you in this first instance, but hey, if not don't worry about it as they may indeed become a customer in the near future. Continue to build a relationship with them with low-pressure communication.

Don't Be a Pushy Sales Person

I expect you've had a conversation with a sales rep at some time or another, who has telephoned you to try to sell you something. You can sense that there is no passion, no enthusiasm, and no real interest in you by the tone of their voice. They just want to sell you something so that they can make some money in commission, which you can sense instantly. On the other hand how would you feel if that sales person went the extra mile and did whatever it took to make *your* life easier, to understand and solve *your* problems, to add value to *your* life, to decipher *your* troubles and meet *your* requirements – wouldn't you just love it!

So many of us switch off when that impending sales phone call comes through. We're just not interested. And why aren't we interested? Because it's the same old thing – pushy sales person blabbering on about how magnificent their service or product is and how much we need it. How does he or she know whether we need it or not? Have they asked any questions to find this out? Probably not. So what do we do – well we switch off and try to tell the sales person about four or five times that we're just not interested. They then become all defensive and ask why we're not interested and they then take it as a personal insult! Eventually you'll put the phone down and mutter to yourself on how rude that pushy sales person was. If you can even begin to remember what company they were representing, that indeed will make you feel a negative pre-disposition towards it. Think about a recent telephone call that you have gotten from a sales rep recently. Before you read on, take a minute or two to think about all the aspects that you disliked about these high-profiled sales calls.

Were your answers

- The sales rep was reading from a script, sounding like a robot and making you feel just like a random telephone number.
- The sales reps opening line was that it was just a courtesy call. Rubbish. It's wasn't a courtesy call it was a sales push.
- The sales rep was being really pushy and not taking no for an answer, and even worse when they questioned you on why you were saying no to them (as if it's any of their business).
- The sales rep was making false claims and lying to you. There is no such thing as a free cruise, a free timeshare and a free £5000.
- The sales rep puts the phone down on you without even saying thank you for your time and goodbye. How rude!

Now think about all the things that you like and admire when a decent sales rep calls, such as:

- The call was significant to you. They made a point to inform you that there is something in it for you. It has value.
- They asked you questions and they actually listened to your answers and then answered and reacted accordingly.
- They let you speak and they never butted in over the top of your words.
- They came straight to the point and didn't beat about the bush with fluffy sales talk.

In our face painting business we don't want to be that pushy sales person, we don't want to intimidate our customer into purchasing and we certainly don't want to get a bad reputation for being too sales-y. We do, however, want to be conceived as understanding our customers' needs, wants and desires, and we do want our reputation to soar due to the value that we are able to provide.

I'd like to share with you a conversation that took place on the phone between me and a soft-play centre just a couple of weeks ago:

Her: Hello – I understand you do face painting
Me: Yes that's right, how can I help?

Her: Oh that's really great because I thought I'd contact you to let you know about our fantastic package that we're doing We have an extremely large footfall of people coming in during the day to our soft-play centre, and after school and to our birthday parties and to our family events that we put on and quite often we do two for the price of one, and sometimes we give the Mum's free coffee. *(She takes a well needed breath and continues with):* We're also doing loyalty vouchers for our customers and monthly memberships. We also send out a newsletter with all the promotions that we're running for that month and also send them a list of the companies that are geared towards party entertainment in the area.

(Okay so we're getting down to it now, here comes the sales pitch, however it's all been about them so far and not once have I heard what's in it for me):

She continues: Our customers can go onto our website and click on a link that will take them straight to your website. Now there's a charge for this *(oh you don't say)* and we can do it for only £3 per week – that's only £150 per year. I don't need to take your payment over the phone today *(oh that's really good of you)* as we can set up a direct debit.

Me (finally get a word in edgeways): Well thank you for phoning but I'm not really interested at this moment in time.

Her: My sales advisor is in your area tomorrow *(yeah right)* and she'll come over to see you and tell you all about it.

Me: Err no thank you – like I just said it's not for me at the moment. Maybe you could email me the details and I can look over the proposal and contact you if I'm interested.

Her: Well no we won't be able to email you anything but you can pop in anytime tomorrow to our centre and speak to our advisor and she'll tell you all about it *(strange, thought you said she was in my area tomorrow)*.

Me: No thank you, I'm really not interested. Goodbye.

Now this conversation could have gone so much better. I could have actually been very interested as it's a place where my target market hang out. Not once during the phone conversation did she explain any of the benefits to my company of which there would have been loads. Not once did she ask how my needs through advertising with them could be met. Not once did she ask for any information on my company and the advertising that I was currently involved with. It was all so one-sided and the focus was on how much it was going to cost me!

Next time you get one of those very annoying phone calls from a pushy sales person, as soon as it's finished make notes on all the aspects of the conversation that displeased you, that were irritating to you and that were just generally unprofessional. Look at your notes and think about how you could have scripted the conversation better. Maybe there were beneficial opportunities that the sales rep totally missed that could have helped with their selling process to you. Use this as a learning curve for your business and avoid making the same mistakes as they did.

Customers Love a Guarantee

Whether it's in your sales process, on your website or on a sales letter that you send out - customers love safety-nets, especially in today's economy. I'm sure you understand that, and also that it's totally acceptable from the customer's point of view that they should have one too. So with this in mind you should be offering your customers a no-brainer, guarantee.

By adding a guarantee you will have put a full risk reversal in place for the customer. A lot of big high street stores like M&S do this and they do it very well. It's their trusted business module. Customers have no risk when they buy from them with their money back guarantee that they have in place.

Have a solid guarantee in place for people who book your service and give your customer risk reversal as you should cover the risk and not them. It's the right thing to do and this will give you strength to sell well, providing you with weight. We used this strategy in our children's party venue and in our face painting business - if at the half way stage of their party they are not completely satisfied with our service we would give them a full refund, yes a full refund. Hand on heart – we have never given a refund because no-one has ever asked for one. So go on - try this out for your business.

CHAPTER 15

Keeping Customers Informed

Don't Leave Customers in The Dark

By keeping customers informed in any areas that you feel may be of interest to them, and in line with your own business style, will most certainly create an expert status about you, and their confidence in you will grow as you position yourself as a trustworthy expert in the face painting industry.

Maybe you read an industry trade magazine, if so you'll find that these publications are a fantastic source of information for you to use and to pass onto your customers. Filled with articles on the latest this and that, the hottest products on the market and the newest style of face painting designs can all be used to keep your customers up-to-date and in the know.

However articles of interest, and snippets of information that you pass on to your customers don't necessarily need to be all about what you already do, or all about what you already sell. Quite the opposite in fact, as to share information with another that clearly has no immediate benefit to you will only serve to enhance your reputation. So keep a look out for articles of interest from fashion and beauty magazines as well.

A short email or text to your customer could read along the lines of:

'Hey (name), I've just been reading my magazine and a fantastic new line of glitter tattoos have just been launched. Thought of you immediately as I'm sure they'll be very popular at your next company event that you're arranging'.

Treat the way you send this information out as if you were chatting to a best friend and keep a conversation tone going with your emails rather than trying to send out a formal editorial piece which could be off-putting. The above example can be sent out to a specific target group or to a specific person. It's also possible to send out a generic message or email to your complete database, especially through your Facebook page and this could be worded as follows:

'Just seen an advert for a competition on the XYZ website to win a luxury day at a National Spa. It's a fantastic offer and the entry for the competition is a cinch. We could all do with some additional pampering to soothe our hectic lives don't you agree'. Then include the link to the competition or article.

Now those types of messages that you send out may not have any immediate benefit to you whatsoever, but there is a benefit to be had. It could quite simply serve as a memory jogger to a customer who has been meaning to give you a call to make a booking but hasn't quite got round to doing it. Your email is there sitting in her inbox and it will be so very easy for her to reply to you and say "Oh thanks for that, glad you contacted me because I've been meaning to phone you to book you in for my daughter's party". This is a win-win situation!

So next time you're flicking through a magazine don't just look at products and services of interest to you, think outside the box (or as we do we think outside of the paint pot) and look for adverts and articles that could be of interest to your customers in a way that you can help to solve a problem of theirs, and the benefit to you will draw that much closer.

Adding to Your Repertoire

Most wealth in business comes from copying other successful businesses already out there in the market place. It's so much more difficult to think of absolutely brand new ideas and you certainly don't want to re-invent the wheel. That's why I'm such an advocate of reading influential business books in order to learn from others, networking at business seminars and attending courses and plenty of webinars.

Maybe now you're in a position where you're comfortable and confident with the services that you already provide to your customers, regardless as to whether that is a small select range or a substantial diverse assortment, and eventually there will come a time when you will want to reach out to add other services to your repertoire.

To get the very best chance of business growth, and for your business to succeed, it's so important to keep up-to-date with current trends as they materialize as our industry moves very, very fast. By offering your customer an up to date face painting design range will ensure that you stay in the forefront of your field and this in turn will accelerate your reputation. Don't let your face painting designs become stale and old fashioned as customers just love to be on the receiving end of something new, something innovative and something extraordinary so that they can brag about it at the school gates amongst their friends. Gaining knowledge and experience in any additional skill-set or product line is the essential key to growth. You'll never know everything there is to know about the services that you provide or the products that you use, it's impossible, because time doesn't stand still and every day new ways of doing things are being introduced and new and improved products lines are coming on to the market.

The very best face painters in the industry, in the World in fact, still strive to improve their skills; they still attend training in specialised areas and make every effort to become familiar with the benefits of latest and up-to-the-minute products to hit the wholesale market. Even if you only choose to attend a one-day training course to advance your capabilities, you'll find that you will be completely re-energised within your business and you'll be inspired to add your newly acquired skill to your range as soon as you can. It's also never too late to once again return to an evening class run by your local college to gain further qualifications in other areas of the hair or beauty industry such as nail art, spray tanning and henna that you can offer as an additional and complementary service.

When I started my face painting company back in 1990, it was just that – a face painting company. Over the first couple of years and once I had a team of staff on board I could see the value to my customers in adding additional services on a broader scale. Over the last two decades I have added glitter tattoos, painted on tattoos, fake wounds, hair braiding and plaiting, coloured hair extensions, henna bodyart, airbrush tattoos, body painting and most recently baby bump painting. I always pushed to make my business bigger and better by capitalising on what I thought my customers would be wanting the next season at their parties, corporate events or shows and festivals that I attended, and I usually got it just right.

Complacency can be a very easy trap to fall into, and if you're not careful one day you may wake up to smell the coffee and realise that the World has moved on and not waited for you. Services, products and equipment can become out-dated as the new, the improved and the more beneficial emerge, and if your competitors are always one step ahead of you that could be the end of your business. So jump on the gravy train and keep on learning, and then after that learn some more!

Bringing New Services on Board

How often do you have one of those moments, when an 'Ah Ha' thought pops into your mind? You may become excited about the prospect of a new service to provide, or a new promotion that you can offer or a new product to sell. You put a lot of effort into the thought process behind this idea, analysing the significant profitable outcome – but in fact you may spend little or no time in actually putting it into practice and getting the thing going, only to despair when someone else does before you!

This is a case of analysis paralysis again.

Spending too much time in the thought process, mulling this and that over, time and time again, can lead to the new idea never even getting off the ground. Now I'm not saying here to just jump straight in with every conceivable idea you may have as that would just be too erratic, instead you should plan out a strategy for the launch of any new concept.

Your launch strategy could go something like this:

- Light Bulb Moment – make notes on paper to capture the thought before it's gone forever
- Research the idea, the product, or the service to get as much information as necessary to take it forward
- Check out its viability – is it something that your prospective customer needs, wants or desires
- What is the end result that the customer will experience and the benefit to them?
- Will it be conceived as a fad, a passing phase, or will it be here to stay?
- Work out the pricing strategy of how much it will cost to put it in place, how much you can sell it for and what are the profit margins?
- Decide on the best marketing angle to get it off the ground quickly
- Then JDFI, before anyone else does!

You don't have to spend countless hours on each of the above points as just a general overview will suffice. As long as you have all the important information covered you can take your idea forward as soon as you feel confident enough to do so. There is no time like the present and unfortunately time stands still for no-one. Get your new service, promotion or product out there as quick as you can and then you can move onto the next one. Don't become a victim to that analysis paralysis, which put another way means 'all talk and no action'. I expect you've come across a lot of people like that – those are the ones who say to you "Yeah, well I was going to do that but just didn't get round to doing it".

As the old saying goes "There are those that do, there's those that don't and there's those that watch others do".

Up Selling and Cross Selling Isn't Rocket Science

How often have you placed an order with a company over the telephone and they have offered you an 'up-sell' – quite often I would expect. You know the kind I mean – you buy a wall clock and they ask if you'd like batteries, you purchase a burger and they say 'fries with that' or you fork out for a new television and they ask if you'd like to purchase an extended warranty. This is up-selling, a very effective marketing strategy.

You need to be in a position where you can do the same for your customer as there is always a great deal of additional income to make from this great little marketing approach. Your up-sell can simply be an additional mini bonus service to add to the main service they are purchasing. You may choose to do a special offer limited for this month only, or a product or service that will compliment what they are buying or increasing the opportunity to pay for painting fifteen children instead of ten at their party (bit like bumping up from a regular size milkshake to a jumbo size milkshake). There are so many different opportunities of up-sells to be had; you just need to be creative in your thinking and decide what it is that you can present to your customer. When I had my fairytale party venue, up-selling was offered to every single customer as normal practice that made a booking with us and more often than not they would purchase additional items such as balloons, party bags and birthday cakes. We even up-sold our regular Princess Party Hostess to Cinderella, Belle and Snow White. I would hazard a guess here and say that at least 85% of our customers purchased an up-sell of some sort to add onto their party. If my staff hadn't been trained to offer these up-sells at the time the customer made the party booking, they would have purchased most of those items somewhere else and I would have lost the additional income to another shop. There is no reason why you too can't offer your party customers such items as balloons, party bags, birthday cake and tableware or venue decor.

Something else not to neglect is cross selling, which means to sell something that has an opposite connection to the product or service that they are buying. An example would be to sell a face painting party and cross-sell a small face painting kit that the birthday child could play with after her event and likewise with glitter tattoos.

You could even produce an up-selling and cross-selling matrix that can be shown on your website where customers can choose their up-sell or cross-sell package to suit their requirements and needs. Package what you offer and give choices on rates as not all customers will be looking for the same outcome, so tailor to a variety of needs to maximize the best possible offers that you can. By offering and promoting up-sells and cross-sells will produce more sales to improve your cash flow and the added bonus is it doesn't cost anything more in advertising as there is no need to invest in new customers to do it – you do it to the customers you've got. Put in up-sells and cross-sells wherever and whenever you can for another win-win situation.

Special Promotions and Incentives to Buy

People just love to bag a bargain, especially the elite kind. So how about offering your customer something that is that little bit extra special, or has money off for a set period or even to launch a brand new and exciting service. You'll find that your customers will be most responsive to give you a call to make a booking.

There are so many different ways that you can offer a special promotion when you think about it. Why not offer an elite package by giving them something special for their birthday, give away the first five of something for free for a written testimonial or offer a discounted price for a set period of time.

These types of marketing activities will be adding money to your bank and by taking the time to put some great elite packages into place will support your business success.

CHAPTER 16

Testimonials

Collecting Influential Social Proof

If you've been in business for at least a year you should have at least six good testimonials. If not, why not? How many testimonials did you capture this month, written or verbal, and to what advantage are you using this influential social proof.

Are you making use of the positive things that your customer has to say about you? If not, then you need to start compiling a database of testimonials, the powerful written words of others. No matter how much time and effort you have put into the words and sentences of your sales materials, no one says it better about you than how your customer says it. Testimonials are perceived as the pure facts about your service or product; they wouldn't make it up, fabricate it or elaborate on the truth like the wordings of an advert may appear to be.

No One Says it Better Than Your Customer

Nothing you ever do, nothing you ever say or nothing you ever write about your face painting business will have more impact or power than that of a testimonial from one of your customers. Testimonials, your influential social proof, will be able to communicate the quality of your service far better than you ever can from people who have experienced your service first-hand. And what's more – they're FREE! So how do you go about harnessing that good-will and accumulating authentic testimonials from your customers? Well simply put - you ASK for them!

Use a guest book (just like those you can buy for Weddings) to leave out on a table at your parties and events. This is an ideal tool as it looks good with its quality cover and has plenty of pages for your customer's to write on, in date order. People can flick through and read what others have had to say about you, and then they can leave their own comments. Nine times out of ten they will add their own testimonial as satisfied customers are only too pleased to provide you with one, so don't be shy about being forthcoming. You should plan to make collecting them an integral part of your business activities, so take your book with you wherever you provide your service and don't forget to leave out a pen!

Testimonials don't just have to be written words either. Another great one is a video testimonial from a satisfied parent or a bunch of kids taken immediately after you have provided your service to them. Capture the excitement and enthusiasm as it happens and add the video to your website, or upload it to Google or to Youtube with a link back to your site. When recording or photographing children, be sure to ask the parent to complete an internet/photographic disclaimer form which will keep you on the right side of the Data Protection Act. For more information on this go to the ICO (Information Commissioners Office) website.

Spontaneous testimonials are also collectable as well. If a customer says something in passing or praises you for your work, then ask if you can quote what she has just said in your marketing materials and write it down word for word at your earliest opportunity.

When out on location at an event you should have your testimonials on show, at the ready for your customers to read whilst they are queuing. They should be focused on you and your business and the benefits that you can offer them. Have on show scrapbooks of information about your business, what you can offer, what you have achieved and most importantly what your customers are saying about you. Your testimonials need to be specific to the service, the product or the business in general and relate to the benefits completely.

Your best testimonial will be one that gives a detailed description of the service or product that you have provided. This testimonial will go into depth, it will report on your professionalism, your standards, and your value for money and maybe your environment. This testimonial captures all the benefits that you offer, and these benefits will have massive impact and are priceless. During an event you could ask your customer what feels special about the particular service they are receiving today and how is it benefiting them. If you ask after you have provided your service try questions like how satisfied were they at doing business with you today. The more explicit the comment the better as 'It was great' as an answer won't prove a thing about your competency. On the other hand 'I am so pleased I booked the XYZ Face Painter as she was very prompt and organised from the onset and she interacted fully with each and every child as she painted them, making each one of the kiddies feel so very special'. As you can see, there are a number of benefits listed here in this testimonial: prompt, organised, interacted fully, each child felt special. You can then take each of those words and use them to write your headlines and sales material.

One of the best testimonials you could possibly have is a celebrity endorsement. Hard to come by I know, but well worth pursuing if you can get someone of important statue to use your service and then write an endorsement about it. If you know of a celebrity that lives in your town (even just a C-listed one) that has children you need to follow them on Twitter or Facebook. Start replying to their tweets or posts they make and get into as many conversations as you can with them over a period of time. Eventually you can start dropping little hints in a subtle way during these conversations about the services that you offer for birthday parties. As you gradually build brand recognition, hey-presto they might look to seek you out for their next party or event, and there you'll have a celebrity endorsement.

You may find it more comfortable to collect testimonials after the customer has had a chance to reflect on the service provided. If this is the case then you could give the customer a stamped addressed postcard that she can take away with her to complete and send back in to you at a later date. The return of postcards on this type of system can sometimes be quite low though and that's why producing a customer satisfaction survey whilst the booker is still in your company is the most effective way. Use open questions here to avoid them from just ticking boxes or just writing 'yes' or 'no'. This type of survey is a good exercise for capturing customer's thoughts.

If you send a personal thank you email to all of your customers after you have provided your service to them your customer will probably reply back to you with some sort of comment, appraisal or review about your service which you can then use. After I've provided my face painting training to each and every customer I will send them an email thanking them for using Mimicks as a training provider. Nearly always they will reply thanking me for the course which tends to be accompanied with a fantastic testimonial.

Make sure that all the testimonials you use have the person's permission, or the company's permission to be used in your promotional activities. The full name of the customer ideally should be shown along with the town or city in which they are from. Testimonials without this information, especially anonymous ones, will hold no value at all and will be considered made-up and totally useless.

You can never have enough testimonials and you should never stop asking for them. As new ones come in these can replace any that have become a little outdated so that your marketing material is always kept fresh. A customer's testimonial will help you to convince people of the promises that you make about your activities, and the words coming from others in the form of a testimonial will most certainly add value to your business. You can further establish your credentials by mentioning other businesses that you've carried out work for.

Go through all your old drawers and cupboards where maybe you have stuffed away some valuable reviews or hand-scribbled notes (that you were going to do something with one day), brush off the dust, and start building your priceless information resources.

- Type out all the testimonials that you already have into a Word Doc in readiness to be pasted into your website

- Purchase a nice guest book and start the ball rolling where you can capture testimonials from your forthcoming customers

- Create a scrapbook of combined information to leave out for your guests to mull over whilst they are waiting for you, or to be served.

The above task will need time and effort on your part – but once achieved you will have some valuable marketing tools that you can use in many different ways, time and time again.

Even if you are just starting out and have no customers yet, provide your face painting service for free to family and friends and then capture the kind words of encouragement that they offer. These testimonials will start you off quite nicely.

Use your testimonials anywhere and everywhere your prospective customer will be looking, including your advertising, your sales literature, your display banner and even on your t-shirt! Use short phrased ones on your business cards and use a wealth of your longer phrased ones throughout the pages of your website. In fact everywhere and anywhere that you know your prospective customer will be looking. Take a look at any of the Mimicks Websites and you'll see testimonials in abundance, working their magic! So go for it, start collecting them today or retrieve those that you have stuffed away in a drawer somewhere, and use them everywhere you possibly can! Make better use of your testimonials – you worked hard for them, so put them absolutely everywhere.

CHAPTER 17

Your Golden Opportunities

Looking For Those Lucky Breaks

You may be in the initial start-up stage of your business or have been going for a number of months or years but I'm sure that you'll more or less be of the same mindset as me that running a business is all about keeping up with current trends, products and services and being in a position to act on those ideas for expansion as soon as they come to light. With the vast amount of information that is ready for us to grab and capitalise on, can sometimes make it difficult to spot an opportunity that can in fact be sitting right under our noses.

As your face painting business grows look for opportunities wherever and whenever you can. You need to keep an open mind and not have tunnel vision just to suit yourself. Look, listen and learn and by doing this you'll open up a whole area of opportunities just waiting to be acted upon. Golden opportunities are everywhere around you and not only can they present themselves when you are having a conversation with a customer, you should also be on the lookout for ideas from unusual sources.

Here are a few opportunity spotters to think about:

- Read a random magazine that you haven't read before as you'll never know what you'll come across that could be turned into a golden opportunity

- Travel to an event via an unusual route to see the neighbourhood or surrounding areas from a different perspective. You might see an advertising bill-board that gets you thinking about a new marketing angle

- Strike up a conversation with someone that you normally wouldn't pass the time of day with, like a taxi driver, the little old lady waiting at the bus stop or the sales assistant in the bakery

- Listen to a different radio station than normal, especially a talk show one

- Watch a different news channel

- Watch a couple of hours of breakfast television occasionally and see what pops up

- Join a network group of like-minded people and rub shoulders with as many people as you can there from a completely diverse range of companies

At the beginning of each working day, read the above list and as you go through the day you'll gradually start to focus on opportunities as and when they arise. By doing this and opening yourself up to situations that are different from the norm, you'll be extending your creative mind and somewhere along the line you'll say, "Ah, now that's a good idea, maybe I could do that too". Be open minded with everything and everyone and something good is sure to materialise!

You could also start with taking a long hard look at your business and where it stands now. Think about areas that are available to you which will add value to your customer's lives by starting with your existing product or service:

- Can you improve your existing product or service?
- Can you enhance your systems in any way?
- Can you obtain a grant or an award?
- Can you make better arrangements with your suppliers?
- Can you speed up your customer booking process?
- Can you obtain new contact sources?
- Can you devise original and enhanced ways of doing absolutely everything in your business?
- Is there anything in your industry that is old fashioned and obsolete? Can you update it?
- Can you devise a back-end product to a service that you provide either at a discounted price or as a free give-away?
- Can you improve your existing service by keeping it at the same price but having the benefits of being advanced or to the standard of a deluxe version?

Get your customers talking. Lead them into conversation but most importantly, listen to what they have to say. See if you can spot how they make their buying decisions and in what conditions. Casual conversations can in fact harvest something useful that you may have never discovered. Take a little test at the end of each week to help you re-focus and you may very well spot something that has been there all along:

- Who has spoken and presented me with an opportunity today?
- What are my customers telling me, what are they saying that they want and need?
- What is there an increased need for at this moment in time?
- What service or product would my customers buy today if I could offer it to them?
- What is different about my business / customer / industry / competitor this week/month?

Every business owner needs thinking time. Day-dreaming as it can be known. I need thinking time to effectively move my business forward. Planning, organising in my head, system building in my mind. Your thinking time should be done in a quiet place and definitely not in front of the TV or with any other distraction.

Golden Opportunities are everywhere. What are your customer's needs? What do they want? How can you give it to them and add massive value to their lives?

Think about it.

Creating a Face Painting Fan Club

It's one thing getting new customers and a completely different thing in keeping them. It takes time, effort and money in order to get each and every one of your customers and if you don't have some sort of system in place for making them stay loyal to you they'll be here today and gone tomorrow, especially your B2B ones.

Systems for customer retention will need to be put in place so that you can consistently monitor the effects that the impact of their profits can have on your business bank account. If you solely rely on a handful of customers to see you through and something changes in unforeseen circumstances to withdraw them from using you as their service provider, what impact will that have on you and your standard of living. Such circumstances could be anything from a new face painter targeting your market, your nearest competitor drastically reducing their prices or the cost of your overheads increasing forcing you to put your prices up. As well as building a customer database you also need to be building a 'fan' database. This is for the type of customer that is very loyal to you and your company. I have a very large B2B 'fan' base that has been built over a considerably long time, and some of my corporate bookers have been loyal to Mimicks for over two decades. Now that's a fan club.

So how do you get customers to become part of your raving fan base? Easy, you make them feel really, really special by doing certain things for a select few of them and treat them like royalty. Before you can start to build your fan base you need to take a long hard look at your customer database in the first instance and ask yourself the following questions of each and every one of them:

- Do I have a good rapport with this company?
- Have we built up a good level of trust between us?
- Have they been consistent with their run of bookings so far?
- Are they willing to try out my new services when launched?
- Do they have a good account history with me?

When looking at each individual customer on your list, if you can honestly answer yes to each of the above questions – then without a doubt they need to be targeted for your raving fan base. So with your raving fan base built, which might incidentally be only about 20% of your overall customer list, it's now time to put some marketing strategies in place for them.

Start by informing them that as a loyal customer you are setting up an 'elite' club for a few of your best customers to be part of and that they have been invited to join (for no charge of course). People like things that are elite as it makes them feel special to be part of something that not everyone can get their hands on, whether that's a bottle of wine, a cocktail dress or a membership to a sailing club. Next have some sort of brochure printed that will outline the benefits to your fan base – making sure that they are all benefits or it will be a pointless exercise.

The benefits could include discounts on all future services that they book with you, price reductions on any of your retail product ranges, information on your new services planned well before your general customers get heed of them, a complimentary pub lunch voucher for four people or a Christmas pamper hamper.

The list above is just a starter and is not exhaustive as you can be as generous as you see fit to lavish your raving fans with whatever you so desire, within reason. Remember that this special little elite club is all about making them feel truly valued as a customer of yours and that they are indeed being rewarded for their loyalty to you.

Just remember the reciprocation rule here – the more you give the more you'll get in return. I'm a strong believer in What Goes Around – Comes Around.

CHAPTER 18

Keep On Moving On

What Will Make You Stand Out From The Rest

If you have even the slightest thought of sitting back, through despondency or boredom, it's time to revisit your objectives as to why you're actually in business and give yourself a kick-start in the right direction to get yourself on track with this wonderful experience you're having being your own boss. Maybe you have a good solid base of customers now and are able to employ someone to help you service them on a part-time basis, maybe you need a virtual assistant to help you with the business administration or maybe it's time to start working on your business a bit more rather than in your business 24/7.

No matter how busy you are in the day to day running of your face painting business you should always take time for 'thinking time' or day-dreaming as it can also be known. We all need thinking time to plan and organize effectively in order to move our business forward. Your thinking time ideally should be done in a quiet place and preferably not in front of the television or with any other distraction to stifle your imaginative impulses.

Creating ideas and building on them is fairly easy and most of us are capable of doing that, when we are in one of those daydreaming modes. The difficulty comes in putting those ideas into practice, seeing the challenges that each idea will possess and working out the path around the idea and its obstacles to its fruition.

Your inspirational ideas will often come to you when you're not at work, when you're relaxing and sometimes from the most unusual situations. This is because you are in a different mindset, away from the working environment and you're looking at things through a different perspective. My inspiration moments come when I am in bed at night, when I'm reading a book and when I'm walking my dogs. This is a relaxing time for me and my mind seems to work ten to the dozen and new ideas just keep popping into my head. Sometimes the ideas come so fast that I trip over them, and feel disappointed if I haven't got a pen and pad to hand to write them down. I now keep a notepad on my bedside table and will reach over and scribble things down so I don't forget them. If I don't, you can bet your bottom dollar that when I awake I can't for the life of me remember the remarkable script for a sales letter that I concocted to myself before nodding off!!

So with all the hustle and bustle that takes place when you're running your business it's important to find a little bit of thinking time at your very own inspiration location, where you can be on your own for a short while each day. This is a valuable time to revisit and contemplate any golden opportunities that customers may have presented to you through conversation along with any exciting ideas that you may have swimming around in your head which will help to move your business forward. Time allocated needn't be long for this process, as at least fifteen minutes daily will be enough for you to jot down notes as memory joggers that can be expanded on at a later date after you have added them to your 'to do' lists.

I've had many missed opportunities over the years and unfortunately I only have myself to blame for not being quicker off the mark! You may have once said, or heard someone say "Yeah well I was gonna do that". It's the classic case of someone beating you to your idea. If you don't write down your thoughts, ideas, hunches and instincts as soon as you can, they may be lost forever – that is until the time that your competitor has the same ones as you had and you turn a nasty shade of green!

Take action in your ideas, tasks, projects and key areas today. Don't hesitate and put off until tomorrow. Never use the "Oh I'm just too busy to do that" Time is the foundation on how everything works as timing is the difference between salad and garbage (probably my most favourite quote)!

To Delegate or Not To Delegate

To delegate or not to delegate – that is the question. You know that you are running your face painting business just as you would like to, and often think that you are the only one that can do certain tasks, sort certain problems and provide certain administration input successfully. In most cases you're probably right. Sometimes, however, things just get a little on top of you and it's the usual scenario of 'so much to do and so little time'. You have too many things to do on your list and you find yourself crying out for a helping hand.

There is unfortunately a limit to what you can do alone to become wealthy. You're going to need to get people to do the unproductive work in your business but first make sure you have the right people in place for the work in hand. You must delegate and let go. I know it can be very difficult to let go, but when you take that huge step from being the one who does the business thing to the one who markets the business thing then that is when income will reach a higher platform.

We've just covered ways in how to market your business both off-line and on-line which as you probably realise is a huge area in itself. You need to ask yourself as to whether you'll be able to implement a lot of those strategies if you only have painting time and not administration time available. Getting people around you to respond effectively with delegation is the only way you will be able to free up your time to concentrate on areas of your business that will make you more money, the marketing side.

So how do you start to delegate in order to relieve some of those pressures? How do you let go of some of those tasks that take up too much of your time, or are just too menial or are just plain boring! Well firstly your need to consider all the actions that you have written on your daily, weekly and monthly lists that we discussed earlier and then secondly decide which ones can be outsourced to someone else. An easy way to sift through your tasks is to rate each one accordingly – is it to be done by you, is it too easy, too boring, too time consuming or too difficult.

Let's take some examples here:

A. To be done by you - these actions are probably your marketing activities which inevitably should be done by you. You and only you will have the drive and the enthusiasm to grow your business by using effective marketing tactics. So invest as much of your time where it's needed, where the money is coming from!

B. Too Easy – could your children give you a hand with these actions like cleaning your kit and equipment, or stuffing envelopes for mail shots or leaflets drops in the local neighbourhood?

C. Too Boring – maybe enlist the help of family members to update your mail merge and customer database, to write the envelopes for your mail shots and to do your Internet research.

D. Too Time Consuming -can you afford a PA or VA to send out your confirmation of bookings and invoices, type out your brainstorm notes, update your blogs, Facebook and Twitter posts.

E. Too Difficult -maybe you need paid professional expertise in areas such as accounting and tax returns, business planning, cash flow forecasting, website management and email sequencing.

With certain tasks on your list categorised to the above it's probably time to delegate certain actions on your list to other people – family, friends, a PA or VA, and professional bodies, in order for you to free up more of your time for the more important aspects of running your business and moving it forward.

Delegation can be a very difficult skill to master as we all think we are the only ones who can do a certain job properly as we hear ourselves saying "OMG I would've been better off doing that myself". In some respects that is true, but you need to let go and learn to delegate effectively. To start you need to explain the process of the task that you wish the person to do as a step by step process and give the delegate as much information as possible, including resources that they'll need and where to find them, and the task should then be effectively undertaken to your satisfaction.

Here are some tips to help you make your delegation happen more seamlessly:

- Classify and clarify what has to be done
- Make sure that your delegate understands the task fully
- Explain to the delegate why the task has to be done
- Teach the delegate how the task should be done, broken down element by element
- Make sure that the delegate understands the complete process of what needs to be done
- Set the deadline for the task to be completed by
- Get the delegate to explain the process back to you so that you can be sure that understanding has taken place

Maybe you've tried to delegate before with no success. The problem could have been that you didn't clarify the task properly and that person was left to their own devices. Maybe you didn't take time to check that they really knew what it was that you were asking them to do in the first place. One small point worth remembering here is that it doesn't really matter how long the delegate takes to complete the task (within reason of course) even if you could have done it in half the time, or if they go around the houses in order to complete it, what matters is that the final outcome of the task is what you would expect the standard to be as a finished result.

By freeing up your time and delegating more tasks will allow you to focus on the key growth areas of your business, the wealth creation areas. This will be the marketing side of your business, which ideally you should be investing as much time as possible into. A large proportion of running a successful business lies in the effective ways in which you are going to market it, and all your creative energy and hard work must be put in to that as a number one priority. Number one priority.

Get A Life Outside of Your Business

When all's said and done about making lists, putting effective plans in place and using every moment of your available time efficiently, your work/life balance is key to not only your business success but also your sanity (I do so hate that term work/life balance but I couldn't think of another one to replace it).

We all need to take a break at some time or another, and that may be just a few days doing nothing at all to a full two weeks away in the sun abroad. It's far too easy to become totally blinkered in our business life and taking time out just doesn't seem to happen often enough. We come up with excuses like "How will the business cope without me", "I'm not earning enough money so I can't really afford it" and "If I'm not around to take phone-calls I might miss some important bookings".

Let me tell you that your business *will* survive without you (or for a couple of weeks at least). I know that it's difficult to take time off during the summer months as that is the most lucrative time for us face painters – but other months are available like March and November where the sun still shines. Make a decision to actually include break times in your diary regardless of whether they are just short weekend breaks or for a longer time-span. If they're scheduled in months and months in advance within your diary you'll find a will and a way that your business will still run smoothly in your absence.

So as well as taking those well-earned breaks and holidays each year that you need in order to function more effectively, you should also be looking at things you can do on a daily basis during your working week to achieve improved results.

In order to perform better at work your mind, body and soul needs to be fit and healthy.

Mind – Feed you mind by reading an inspiring article or a chapter of a business book daily and this will make you feel motivated and enthused. Check out all the different types of wholesome foods that you can eat to help with your mental functions as well.

Body – You shouldn't sit for too long especially working at your desk (tell me about it as I've been sat at this computer for nine hours already today), so move around every forty-five minutes. It's amazing how much I feel stimulated and refreshed after a quick trot around the block to blow away the computer cobwebs.

Soul – How about feeding your soul by doing something that is for you and only you, and in no way business driven. This can include relaxation, yoga, listening to music, going shopping, gardening, swimming, spending time with friends you don't see very often. Do something other than working in and on your business that makes you feel good leaving you with a feeling of accomplishment.

Oh, and don't forget to include all those mind, body and soul activities into your diary time sheets as well, along with all your short-breaks and holidays.

So we've covered quite a lot in this book and I really hope that you feel inspired by what you've read. Perhaps it has given you that much needed push and determination you longed for in order to organise your business ideas, your tasks and pending projects into a more realistic and categorised system so that you can work more productively with the hours that you have available to spend on business growth.

Maybe now you have a clearer picture on what it takes to actually meet the needs that your customer has and how to be more benefit driven in providing a service that your customer actually wants and *not what you think they want*. It could be the right time for you to think more about how you can build an ongoing relationship with them especially in the business to business sector.

Hopefully I have shone some light onto the vast range of opportunities that you have at your fingertips to promote and advertise your business with regards to all of the proven marketing strategies that I have used successfully over the years and have possibly reduced any fears you may have had regarding marketing as a whole and marketing costs. Let me know how you get on, I'm looking forward to hearing from you so please feel free to contact me anytime at sherrill@mimicks.co.uk

And finally I wish you great achievement with all the promising business opportunities that are waiting out there for you to encounter, and as much success as possible in **Growing Your Highly Profitable Face Painting Business.**

Sherrill Church

Face Painting For Profit - Mimicks
An innovative marketing advice club for the
Face Painting industry's business owners – like you

Stuck for marketing ideas, want to get an inside look on how the experts of the industry are doing it or need to ramp up your social media marketing strategies? Then at Face Painting For Profit you will find all the inspiration you could possibly need to help grow you business to its next level. FPFP is a membership club for small business owners just like you where your challenges and reservations are answered by people who have been there, done that. There are plenty of free articles at the club in a variety of topics for you to browse through or you can become a fully-fledged club member and have elite access to additional marketing resources. See you over there. **www.facepaintingforprofit.co.uk**

Resources

Product Suppliers

Mimicks Face Painting
➤ Whether you're a seasoned professional face painter in the industry or have recently started and been bitten by the face painting bug, or even just had your very first inclination to get going in a new and exciting venture - then we have all the face painting products that your heart could possibly desire. The Mimicks team have been face painting for over two decades and have been supplying products to the trade for just as long. With an abundance of products available on the market today, the items sold on their website have all be used extensively by Sherrill and Ashlea and a lot are endorsed on the MimicksTV Youtube channel where you can see the products being used to their full glory.
www.facepainting.uk.com

Facade
➤ Your online shop for quality YBODY Glitter and Airbrush Tattoo products, along with the best range of stencils and cosmetic glitters available in the UK. Our stencils, glues and glitters are the preferred choice of professional face and body artists around the world. Try them and you will soon realise why! We also offer a full range of Iwata Compressors, Airbrushes and Body Art products. We are the UK distributor for Cameleon face and body paint.
www.facadebodyart.co.uk

The Face Painting Shop
➤ The Face Painting Shop was set up by professional face painters who have been in the business for over 15 years, working with many celebrities and blue chip companies. We know the best products to stock and are always on hand to help with advice and tips. We are your one-stop shop that stocks the full ranges of Superstar, Snazaroo, Diamond FX, Silly Farm, ShowOff body art stencils and Charles Fox.
www.thefacepaintingshop.com

SillyFarm

➤ SillyFarm is the largest specialized store for everything face and body art, catering to the needs of all sorts of artists. Whether you are a novice face painter or an experienced body painter Silly Farm has what you want and need. With a team of twenty seven employees, that are talented painters in their own right, they are eager and willing to help you reach your face and body art goals. Each staff member has extensive product knowledge and can guide you through the 5,000 products we carry.

www.sillyfarm.com

Dauphines

➤ We are a supplier of top-quality makeup and wigs and have been in the theatrical business for a generation providing theatres, operatic societies, drama groups, face painters and the public alike. Our ranges include water-based makeup, cream makeup, camouflage make-up, brushes and glitter... you name it, we supply it, Nationally and Internationally as well.

www.dauphines.co.uk

Training Providers

Mimicks Face Painting

➤ Mimicks Courses in Face Painting, Henna Body Art, Glitter Tattoos and Casualty Make-up have the potential to be of great value should you be seeking a new hobby or interest, as well as increasing your income stream. Each course explores what it will take for you to apply creative make-up techniques and the importance of using the correct products and equipment to improve your skills. Consisting of fully comprehensive, practical and rewarding sessions will provide you with the expert advice necessary to get you started.

www.facepaintingtraining.com

Facade

➤ The Facade Academy of Face and Body Art is located in a superb modern facility at the Paradise Wildlife Park in Hertfordshire. Our courses include Face painting for all levels and specialties, Body Painting, Introductory Course in Airbrushing and we have occasional courses by guest instructors who are at the top of their game.
www.facadebodyart.co.uk

Treasure House – The Make-up Academy

➤ Our focus is to provide makeup artists and students with the necessary skills for their professional advancement within the Cosmetics Industries. We offer a vocational experience guaranteed to satisfy and enhance the training of the most eager and demanding students. All of our courses have been developed with the support and knowledge of industry leaders that incorporate the most up-to-date techniques and products. We provide courses in Body Painting, Airbrushing, Casualty and Special Effects, Fashion and Beauty, TV and Film. Visit our website today for more information.
www.treasurehouseofmakeup.co.uk

Capital Hair and Beauty

➤ We are a hair and beauty wholesaler who offer a wide range of accredited make-up, beauty and hair courses using both local independent specialists and national training companies. Our aim is to give you affordable and professional hair and beauty training in your area combined with an enjoyable and fun day that will give you another skill or technique to add to your menu.
www.capitalhairandbeauty.co.uk

Tutorial Contributors

Ashlea Henson – Mimicks Face Painting

➤ Ashlea is the creative partner at Mimicks Face Painting and has been producing tutorial videos for a number of years. If you're new to face painting Ashlea will inspire you with just how far you can go in this wonderful creative industry. She enjoys passing on her face painting skills and has a good selection of tutorials aimed at beginners through to the more advanced artistes. Check Ashlea out at:

www.Youtube.com/MimicksTV

FabaTV

➤ Taking online face and body art classes from the world's best instructors has never been easier. You no longer have to take days off of work, travel, find a sitter, or re-arrange your schedule to be able to take face and body art classes. We offer quality training on your time, at your pace, in the comfort of your own home! What more can you ask for? At FABAtv.com can you find classes covering every aspect of face and body art including classes on face painting, airbrushing, Black light body art, marketing, henna, and so much more. Visit them at:

www.fabatv.com

Magazines and Directories

Illusion Magazine

➤ Without a doubt, this is the best printed publication to hit the face and body painting industry. With four editions each year, the magazine is bursting with amazing talent from across the globe. Packed full of original step-by-step artwork, artist features, industry news and reviews, this magazine is for anyone who is interested in face and body art, whether it's their hobby or passion. Illusion's online shop is also a resource in its own right and stocks face and body painting books, DVDs, brushes, kitbags and stencils. Illusion is guaranteed to inspire you.

www.illusionmagazine.co.uk

The Showman's Directory

➤ Our directory is the definitive guide to outdoor events and services. The Showman's Directory was first published in 1968 and over the years has grown into the most comprehensive publication of its kind on the market today listing a calendar of UK outdoor events and contact details of the event organisers, Order one today! Once you've got it you'll wonder how you ever survived without it.

www.showmans-directory.co.uk

Make-up Artist Magazine

➤ Make-Up Artist magazine is read in nearly 70 countries around the world and was created in 1996 by Emmy Award-winning make-up artist Michael Key. The magazine features articles on the entertainment industry's top make-up artists, the most innovative make-up techniques, current product news and invaluable information available nowhere else. The art of make-up branches in many directions and this magazine covers them all so creatively.

www.makeupmag.com

Progressive Party

➤ The definitive source of information for all those in the party business. Progressive Party works closely with both party trade associations and trade show organisers to help create as much new business as possible in the party industry. By sharing knowledge and contacts we offer our clients more opportunities than just advertising! Product areas covered include balloons, costumes, partyware, wedding and celebration, masks, party props and scene setting, novelty products and everything in between - no matter how weird and wonderful it may be!

www.progressiveparty.co.uk

Party Party Magazine

➢ Party Party is essential reading for anyone in the party industry. Containing high interest editorial and a discerning readership provides the ideal environment for advertisers to promote their products with confidence.

www.partypartymag.co.uk

Membership and Academy Sites

Face Painting For Profit

➢ Stuck for marketing ideas, want to get an inside look on how the experts of the industry are doing it or need to ramp up your social media marketing strategies? Then at Face Painting For Profit you will find all the inspiration you could possibly need to help grow you business to its next level. FPFP is a membership club for small business owners just like you where your challenges and reservations are answered by people who have been there, done that. There are plenty of free articles at the club in a variety of topics for you to browse through or you can become a fully-fledged club member and have elite access to additional marketing resources. See you over there.

www.facepaintingforprofit.co.uk

Face Painting Academy

➢ Sometimes being a new face painter in the industry can be quite a daunting prospect in knowing how to get those first birthday parties and company events. The Face Painting Academy is a place where you can be listed as a 'New' face painter looking for work without having the worry factor of skill, speed and longevity in the industry. With every booking that you secure through the Academy will be one step closer in adding to your expertise as a first-class face painter. And better still – a fantastic way for you to promote yourself and your new business to the masses.

www.facepaintingacademy.com

Conventions and Forums

International Face and Body Art Convention

➢ The Face and Body Art International Convention -"FABAIC", is recognized as the original and premier event for the Face and Body Art community. The five-day event in Florida has all the following exciting features that you have come to know and love including cutting edge training, classes for every level and a retail marketplace. FABAIC has it all! There is no better place to learn new skills, increase your network, meet new friends and have the time of your life.
www.fabiac.com

Paintopia

➢ The Paintopia Face Painting and Body Art Festival consists of workshops, competitions, trade stands and demonstrations for Face painters and Body Artists of all calibre. Our retail marquee will host all your favourite paints, glitters and books. The event opens to the general public as well on the Festival Sunday. Held at Dunston Hall in Norfolk, this is one festival not to be missed.
www.paintopia.co.uk

FACE Conference

➢ Each year we hold our Annual Conference in the UK for our FACE members. This provides a great chance for lots of networking with like-minded individuals.
www.facepaint.co.uk

Forums

➢ Forums for face painters.
www.facepaintingchat.co.uk
www.facepaintforum.com

Awarding Bodies

VTCT

> VTCT is the specialist awarding organisation for the hairdressing and beauty sector and the first non-unitary awarding body accredited to offer the Principal Learning for the new Diploma in Hair and Beauty Studies. Our full qualification package also covers complementary therapies, sport and active leisure, business skills and hospitality and catering.

www.vtct.org.uk

City & Guilds

> City & Guilds is a world leading vocational education organisation. We develop vocational qualifications across a variety of sectors that meet the needs of today's workplace, and help individuals develop their talents and abilities for future career progression. Our qualifications are delivered in more than 10,000 training centres across the world and are widely recognised and respected by employers.

www.cityandguilds.com

Insurance and Associations

Rees Astley

> Bespoke cover for the Entertainment Industry. Our Face Painting insurance can cover you for all things that probably will not happen, but might! Our primary focus is on providing cost effective insurance solutions for the self employed operating within defined markets. It's your ideal choice providing peace of mind by giving protection against many of the risks likely to be faced, as well as the flexibility to choose the level and extent of cover to meet individual requirements.

www.insurance4performingarts.co.uk

Blackfriars Insurance Brokers

➤ We offer highly competitive insurance for face painters with full quotations containing all premium information to help you make an informed choice. It is vital for all businesses to carry an appropriate level of liability insurance protection to enable them to defend and meet the costs of claims that maybe made against them whether this is from third parties or employees, clients and members of the public. Our specialist liability insurance team are on hand to assist you with your face painter's liability insurance.

www.blackfriarsgroup.com

FHT – Federation of Holistic Therapies

➤ Professional insurance can be confusing but all practising therapists should have it – that's why the FHT is here to help! As the leading professional association for therapists, and an authorised and regulated insurance intermediary, we really can advise you on the best type Insurance is only available to members of the association.

www.fht.org.uk

FACE – The Face Painting Association

➤ The Face Painting Association is for like minded people to get together and share ideas and problems in order to improve standards and raise the profile of face painting. FACE membership covers the whole of the world and its aims are to meet the needs of its members with the magazine, website and membership directory as well as opportunities to work together. FACE members routinely share their ideas, designs and tips with each other, this allows us to form friendships and be inspired by each other's designs and working methods.

www.facepaint.co.uk

Disclosure Scotland

➢ Should you be required to supply a basic, standard or enhanced disclosure (CRB check) then a self-certified one is available from this organisation. A Disclosure is a document containing impartial and confidential criminal history information held by the police and government departments which can be used by employers to make safer recruitment decisions. Anyone can apply for a basic disclosure in their own name.

www.disclosurescotland.co.uk

Data Protection - ICO

➢ From data protection and electronic communications to freedom of information and environmental regulations, the ICO is the UK's independent public body set up to uphold information rights in the public interest, promoting openness by public bodies and data privacy for individuals. Find out more about our responsibilities and obligations under the legislation we cover here at the Information Commissioners Office.

www.ico.org.uk

The Inland Revenue - HMRC

➢ We are the UK's tax authority. We are responsible for making sure that the money is available to fund the UK's public services and for helping families and individuals with targeted financial support. HMRC's work to make it easy for customers to deal with their taxes and get things right, by making our products and processes more simple and straightforward, and by improving our customer service.

www.hmrc.gov.uk

ABOUT THE AUTHOR

Sherrill Church is the founder of Mimicks Face Painting, which was established in 1990. Most of Sherrill's friends, family and acquaintances were keen to point out to her in those early years that 'face painting was just a fad, give it three years and it'll be over, here today gone tomorrow', and the most insulting comments heard were 'you should get a proper job, you'll never earn any money just face painting'. Well over two decades later business is still booming and Sherrill is now painting 2nd generation customers and she enjoys a satisfying and very financially rewarding lifestyle that can only come from running a successful business that she is still passionately in love with.

Sherrill's year-round working weekends consist of providing creative make-up services such as face painting, glitter tattoos and henna body art at birthday parties, school fetes, community fun-days, and shows and festivals, and is very much in demand at company events for business promotion. Her daughter Ashlea Henson, who was a young child when she started the company, is now a partner in the business and is responsible for the creative side of the company.

During the week Sherrill trains private individuals who are looking to start a face painting company and are in need of learning the basic skills to get them going in this very lucrative and fulfilling business venture. She is also a training provider for one of the large Hair and Beauty Wholesalers and her courses take her across the whole of the UK. Recently she has been providing continued professional development courses for lecturers in colleges teaching them too on how to deliver the Themed Face Painting unit by City & Guilds and VTCT in their own colleges.

People often ask her about the accomplishment and longevity of Mimicks Face Painting and how come it's been so successful over the years. It really is quite simple she says – She just has full-on passion and a strong belief in what she does, loving every moment of this five-minute wonder!

Neither the author or publisher will accept responsibility for any damages or loss that may result from using the ideas, advice or any other information that has been outlined in this book. The outcomes may not be suitable for every situation nor for every person.

The author and publisher make no warranties with respect to accuracy nor suitability of the contents of the work herein and specifically disclaim all warranties of fitness for any particular purpose.

This book is sold on the understanding that neither the author or publisher has rendered full legal advice, accounting advice or service advice as the reader should seek further professional advice where applicable.

24032348R00146

Made in the USA
Charleston, SC
12 November 2013